IBN JUZAYY'S
TAQRĪB AL-WUṢŪL
ILĀ ʿILM AL-UṢŪL

IBN JUZAYY'S
TAQRĪB AL-WUṢŪL
ILĀ ʿILM AL-UṢŪL

Facilitating Access
to the Science of Legal Theory

Shaykh Ibn Juzayy al-Kalbī

Translation with notes by
MUSA FURBER

ISBN   978-1-944904-28-9 (paper)

Published by:
Islamosaic
islamosaic.com
publications@islamosaic.com

All praise is to Allah alone, the Lord of the Worlds
And may He send His benedictions upon
our master Muḥammad, his Kin
and his Companions
and grant them
peace

TRANSLITERATION KEY

ء	' (A distinctive glottal stop made at the bottom of the throat.)
ا	ā, a
ب	b
ت	t
ث	th (Pronounced like the *th* in *think*.)
ج	j
ح	ḥ (A hard *h* sound made at the Adam's apple in the middle of the throat.)
خ	kh (Pronounced like *ch* in Scottish *loch*.)
د	d
ذ	dh (Pronounced like *th* in *this*.)
ر	r (A slightly trilled *r* made behind the upper front teeth.)
ز	z
س	s
ش	sh
ص	ṣ (An emphatic *s* pronounced behind the upper front teeth.)
ض	ḍ (An emphatic *d*-like sound made by pressing the entire tongue against the upper palate.)
ط	ṭ (An emphatic *t* sound produced behind the front teeth.)
ظ	ẓ (An emphatic *th* sound, like the *th* in *this*, made behind the front teeth.)
ع	' (A distinctive Semitic sound made in the middle of the throat and sounding to a Western ear more like a vowel than a consonant.)
غ	gh (A guttural sound made at the top of the throat, resembling the untrilled German and French *r*.)
ف	f
ق	q (A hard *k* sound produced at the back of the palate.)
ك	k
ل	l
م	m
ن	n
ه	h (This sound is like the English *h* but has more body. It is made at the very bottom of the throat and pronounced at the beginning, middle, and ends of words.)
و	ū, u
ي	ī, i, y
ﷺ	A supplication made after mention of the Prophet Muḥammad, translated as "May Allah bless him and grant him peace."

CONTENTS

الْمُحْتَوَيَاتُ

TRANSLATOR'S PREFACE

مُقَدِّمَةُ الْمُتَرْجِمِ]

In the name of Allah the Most Merciful and Compassionate

This book presents Ibn Juzayy al-Kalbī's *Taqrīb al-Wuṣūl ilā ʿIlm al-Uṣūl* (*Facilitating Access to the Science of Legal Theory*). It is a concise introduction to *uṣūl al-fiqh* written in eighth-century Granada; it is one of the most widely studied Mālikī texts in the discipline. Ibn Juzayy composed it as a guide for his son Muḥammad, that the young man might gain a solid footing in legal theory (*uṣūl al-fiqh*), and the title itself signals the author's governing intent: to bring the science near (*taqrīb*) and make it accessible.

ABOUT THE AUTHOR

Abū al-Qāsim Muḥammad ibn Aḥmad ibn Muḥammad ibn ʿAbd Allāh ibn Juzayy al-Kalbī (693–741 AH/1294–1340 CE) was a leading Mālikī jurist, grammarian, and scholar of legal theory from Granada. He studied under a number of prominent scholars, among them the grammarian and *uṣūlī* Abū Jaʿfar Aḥmad ibn Ibrāhīm ibn al-Zubayr al-Gharnāṭī, the *ḥadīth* scholar and Mālikī jurist Abū al-Qāsim ibn al-Shāṭṭ al-Anṣārī al-Sabtī, the *ḥāfiẓ* Ibn Rushayd al-Sabtī, and others including Ibn al-Kammād and al-Ṭanājī. He in turn trained many students, among them his own sons and the celebrated Lisān al-Dīn ibn al-Khaṭīb, who described him as a man devoted to scholarship and authorship, who excelled across multiple disciplines – *fiqh*, *uṣūl*, *ḥadīth*, Qurʾānic recitation, Arabic, and literature – and who was appointed preacher at a young age on account of his universally acknowledged merit.

Ibn Juzayy was a prolific author. His major works include *al-Qa-wānīn al-Fiqhiyyah fī Talkhīṣ Madhhab al-Mālikiyyah, al-Tashīl li-'Ulūm al-Tanzīl* (a well-known Qur'ānic commentary), *Wasīlat al-Muslim fī Tahdhīb Ṣaḥīḥ Muslim, al-Anwār al-Saniyyah fī al-Alfāẓ al-Sunniyyah, al-Fawā'id al-'Āmmah fī Laḥn al-'Āmmah, al-Bāri'* fī Qirā'at Nāfi', *and a large* Fihrist* listing numerous scholars from the eastern and western Islamic worlds.

In 741/1340, he was killed while rallying the Muslim troops at the Battle of Ṭarīf, and has since been remembered as a martyr.

ABOUT THE BOOK

Ibn Juzayy states in his introduction that he relied throughout on brevity and approximation together with sound arrangement and refinement. The work is organised into a preface and five chapters, each containing ten sections, for a total of fifty sections. The five divisions treat, in order: rational knowledge, linguistic knowledge, legal rulings, the evidences for those rulings, and independent reasoning (*ijtihād*), uncritical adherence to authority (*taqlīd*), legal responses (*fatwā*), and the reconciliation and preference of conflicting proofs. Ibn Juzayy explains the rationale for this sequence: since legal rulings are the ultimate object of the science, they are placed before the evidences on which they depend; the rational and linguistic preliminaries are placed first of all because nothing that follows can be understood without them.

Ibn Juzayy's primary source was al-Qarāfī's *Sharḥ Tanqīḥ al-Fuṣūl,* from which he borrowed extensively – at times verbatim. He also drew on al-Ghazālī's *al-Mustaṣfā,* particularly for the division on rational knowledge, where he follows the approach of the *mutakallimūn* and logicians; and on al-Juwaynī's *al-Burhān,* especially in his treatment of reports (*khabar*) and analogy (*qiyās*). Among the works he is thought to have consulted are al-Bājī's *Iḥkām al-Fuṣūl,* al-Bāqillānī's *al-Taqrīb fī Uṣūl al-Fiqh,* Ibn Ḥazm's *al-Iḥkām,* and Fakhr al-Dīn al-Rāzī's *al-Maḥṣūl.*

The work is characterised by several distinctive features. Ibn Juzayy presents the Mālikī position on each issue, then notes the views of the Shāfiʿī and Ḥanafī schools, preferring whichever opinion he judges strongest on the basis of rational and textual evidence. He avoids repetition by means of frequent cross-references between chapters, and he formulates many of his definitions independently rather than simply reproducing those of earlier authorities. He does not, however, engage in extended disputation or detailed refutation of opposing views; his aim throughout is simplification. Uniquely among *uṣūl* authors, he concludes the work with a chapter on the causes of disagreement among the *mujtahids* – a subject he considers essential for strengthening confidence in the results of *ijtihād*, though one that earlier *uṣūlīs* had generally consigned to works of comparative *fiqh*, such as Ibn Rushd's *Bidāyat al-Mujtahid*.

The text has been published in several editions. Among them are the edition prepared by Muḥammad ʿAlī Farkūs, published by Dār al-Aqṣā in Kuwait in 1990; the edition edited by Muḥammad al-Mukhtār ibn Muḥammad al-Amīn al-Shinqīṭī, published in Medina in 2002; the edition edited by ʿAbd Allāh Muḥammad al-Jubūrī, published by Dār al-Nafāʾis in Jordan, also 2002; the edition edited by Muḥammad Ḥasan Muḥammad Ḥasan Ismāʿīl by Dār al-Kutub al-ʿIlmiyyah in Beirut, in 2003.[1]

ABOUT THE TRANSLATION

I have taken the liberty of giving each chapter, section, and subsection a number and referring to its heading; and replacing "As for..." with paragraphing. Notes starting with (Tr:) are from the translator; they may be safely ignored without loss of continuity. I have added

---

[1] Sources: Muḥammad al-Khāḍir, "Taqrīb al-Wuṣūl ilā ʿIlm al-Uṣūl li-Ibn Juzayy al-Kalbī al-Gharnāṭī (t. 741 AH)," Markaz al-Dirāsāt wa-l-Buḥūth fī al-Fiqh al-Mālikī, al-Rābiṭah al-Muḥammadiyyah li-l-ʿUlamāʾ, March 24, 2015, https://www.arrabita.ma/blog/تقريب-الوصول-إلى-علم-الأصول-لابن-جزي-ال/; Al-Khāḍir, "Taqrīb al-Wuṣūl"; "Manhaj al-Imām Ibn Juzayy fī Kitāb Taqrīb al-Wuṣūl ilā ʿIlm al-Uṣūl," Fajr al-Islām (blog), October 23, 2014, http://farj-al-islam.blogspot.com/2014/10/blog-post_7.html.

biographical notes for persons mentioned in the text, as well as an index of technical terms and persons.

* * *

It is my honour to bring this text to English-reading audiences. May Allah bless the author of our text, those mentioned in the text or footnotes, those who contributed in any way to bringing it to English readers, and their fellow readers. And may He forgive the translator and protect readers from his copious shortcomings.

MUSA FURBER
CYBERJAYA, MALAYSIA
1447 AH/2026 CE

SHAYKH IBN JUZAYY AL-KALBĪ'S

FACILITATING ACCESS TO THE SCIENCE OF LEGAL THEORY

Taqrīb al-wuṣūl ilā ʿilm al-uṣūl

O

THE AUTHOR'S INTRODUCTION

مقدّمة المؤلف

بِسْمِ اللَّهِ الرَّحْمَنِ الرَّحِيمِ
صلَّى اللَّه على سيّدنا محمّد وآله وصحبه وسلّم

In the name of Allah, the All-Merciful, the Ever-Merciful
May Allah bless our master Muḥammad, his family, and his
companions, and grant them peace.

قال الشيخ الفقيه الأستاذ العالم أبو القاسم بن أحمد بن جُزيّ رحمه
اللَّه تعالى، وجعل الجنّة مثواه، آمين:

The Shaykh, jurist, teacher, and scholar Abū al-Qāsim ibn Aḥmad
ibn Juzayy – may Allah have mercy on him and make Paradise his
abode, *āmīn* – said:

الحمد للَّه الذي رفع بالعلم درجات أهله، وأجزل ثوابهم على اكتسابه
وعلى نقله، كما أنعم عليهم بالتوفيق لدرسه وحمله، وصلوات اللَّه وسلامه
على سيّدنا محمّد خاتم أنبيائه ورسله، الذي هدى كافة الخلق إلى
منهاج الحق وسبله، وبالغ في تبليغ الرسالة بقوله وفعله، بذل جهده بين
إقامة دين اللَّه وبيان فرعه وأصله، حتى ظهر مصداق قول الملك جل
جلاله: ﴿هُوَ الَّذِي أَرْسَلَ رَسُولَهُ بِالْهُدَى وَدِينِ الْحَقِّ لِيُظْهِرَهُ عَلَى الدِّينِ

كُلِّهِ﴾ [التوبة ٣٣]. ورضي اللَّه عن أهل بيته الطاهرين وأصحابه الأكرمين وحشرنا معهم تحت ظلال عرشه يوم لا ظلَّ غير ظلّه.

Praise be to Allah, who has elevated by knowledge the ranks of its possessors, and has magnified their reward for acquiring it and for transmitting it, just as He has bestowed upon them the grace of being guided to study and bear it. May the blessings and peace of Allah be upon our master Muḥammad, the seal of His prophets and messengers, who guided all creation to the path of truth and its ways, and who exerted himself to the utmost in conveying the message through his speech and action, expending his effort between establishing the religion of Allah and clarifying its branches and its root, until the truth of the saying of the Sovereign – majestic is His glory – became manifest: "He it is who sent His Messenger with guidance and the religion of truth, that He might cause it to prevail over all religion."[2] And may Allah be pleased with his pure household and his noble companions, and gather us with them under the shade of His Throne on the Day when there is no shade but His.

أمَّـا بعـد: فإنَّ العلـوم علـى ثلاثة أضـرب: علم عقلـيّ، وعلم نقليّ، وعلـم يأخـذ مـن العقل والنقل بطرف، فلذلك أشـرف في الشـرف علـى أعلـى شـرف، وهو علم أصـول الفقه الذي امتزج بـه المعقول بالمنقول، واشـتدَّ علـى النظر في الدليل والمدلول، وإنه لنعم العون على فهم كتاب اللَّه وسـنَّة الرسـول -صلَّى اللَّه عليه وسلَّم-، وناهيك من علم يرتقي الناظر فيـه عن حضيـض رتبة المقلّديـن، إلى رفيع درجـات المجتهدين، وأقلّ أحوالـه أن يعـرف وجوه الترجيح فيفرقه بين الراجـح والمرجوح، ويميّز بين السـقيم والصحيح، وإنّي أحببت أن يضرب ابني محمّد -أسعده اللَّه- في هذا العلم بسـهمه، فصنّفت هذا الكتاب برسـمه ورسمته بوسمه، لينشط

لدرسـه وفهمه، وعوّلت فيه على الاختصار والتقريب، مع حسـن الترتيب والتهذيب، وقسمته إلى خمسة فنون:

الفنّ الأوّل: في المعارف العقليّة.

الفنّ الثاني: في المعارف اللغويّة.

الفنّ الثالث: في الأحكام الشرعيّة.

الفنّ الرابع: في الأدلّة على الأحكام الشرعيّة.

الفنّ الخامس: في الاجتهاد والترجيح.

To proceed: Sciences are of three kinds: rational science, transmitted science, and a science that partakes of both reason and transmission.

Therefore, it has thereby towered, in nobility, above the loftiest height of nobility – namely, the science of legal theory (*uṣūl al-fiqh*), in which the rational is interwoven with the transmitted, and which demands rigorous inquiry into proof and what is proven. Indeed, it is an excellent aid for understanding the Book of Allah and the Sunnah of the Messenger – may Allah bless him and grant him peace. What more need be said of a science by which the one who studies it ascends from the lowly rank of the imitators to the lofty degrees of the independent jurists. At the very least, it enables one to know the aspects of preferential weighing (*tarjīh*), distinguishing between the stronger and the weaker, and differentiating between the unsound and the sound.

I have desired that my son Muḥammad – may Allah make him felicitous – take his share in this science. So I composed this book for him and titled it bearing his name, that he might be encouraged to study and understand it. I have relied in it upon conciseness and accessibility, along with good arrangement and refinement.

I have divided it into five arts:

The First Art: On Intellectual Cognitions.

The Second Art: On Linguistic Cognitions.

The Third Art: On the Legal Rulings.

The Fourth Art: On the Evidences for the Legal Rulings.

The Fifth Art: On Independent Juristic Reasoning and Preferential Weighing.

وجعلــت في كلّ فنّ عشــرة أبــواب، فاحتوى الكتاب على خمســين بابًا، وقدّمت في أوّله مقدّمته يحتاج إليها وســمّيته: «تقريب الوصول إلى علم الأصول» واللَّه المستعان.

I have arranged in each art as ten sections, so the book comprises fifty sections.[3] I have placed at its beginning its introduction which one needs, and I have named it: *Bringing Near the Attainment of Legal Theory (Taqrīb al-wuṣūl ilā ʿilm al-uṣūl)*. And Allah is the One whose help is sought.

0.1   ON THE EXPLANATION OF LEGAL THEORY

الفصل الأوّل: في تفسير أصول الفقه

وهو مركّب من كلمتين، فنفسّر كلّ واحدة على انفراد، ثمّ نفسّر المركّب منهما. أمّا الأصول فجمع أصل، وله في اللغة معنيان: أحدهما: ما منه الشــيء والآخر ما يبنى عليه الشــيء حسّــيًّا أو معنى، وله في الاصطلاح معنيان: أحدهما: الراجح والآخر: الدليل.

Uṣūl al-fiqh (legal theory) is a compound of two words. We shall explain each one separately, then explain the compound formed from them.

Uṣūl is the plural of *aṣl*. In language, it has two meanings: that from which a thing comes to be; and that upon which a thing is built, either sensibly or in meaning.

---

3   (Tr): Aside from the introduction, the translation maps each art to a chapter, each *bāb* within it to a section, and each *faṣl* to subsection.

In technical usage, it has two meanings: the preponderant, and the proof.

وأمّا الفقه فهو في اللُّغة الفهم، وهو في الاصطلاح: «العلم بالأحكام الشرعيّة الفرعيّة بأدلّتها على التفصيل في الأحكام وفي أدلّتها».

Fiqh (law), in language, means understanding. In technical usage, it is knowledge of the subsidiary legal rulings of the Sharīʿah, along with their evidences, in detail regarding the rulings and their evidences.

فقولنا: «العلم»، نريد به ما يشمل القطع والظنّ، لأنّ الفقه منه مقطوع به ومظنون، فالعلم هنا الظنّ وما في معناه.

Our statement "knowledge" – by it we mean that which includes certainty and presumption, because law (*fiqh*) comprises both what is certain and what is presumptive.[4] Thus, knowledge here is presumption, and what is akin to it.

وقولنا: «بالأحكام»، تحزّزًا من العلم بالذوات.

Our statement "concerning the rulings" is to guard against [the implication of] knowledge of essences.

وقولنا: «الشرعيّة»، تحزّزًا من العقليّة وغيرها.

Our statement "legal" is to guard against the rational and other such types.

وقولنا: «الفرعيّة»، تحزّزًا من أصول الدين.

Our statement "subsidiary" is to guard against the fundamentals of religion.

وقولنا: «بأدلّتها»، تحزّزًا من التقليد، وهو: «الاعتقاد بغير دليل»، فإنّه لا يُسمّى في الاصطلاح فقهًا.

---

4   See §1.1.

Our statement "with its evidences" is to guard against uncritical adherence to authority (*taqlīd*), which is "holding a belief without evidence,"[5] for it is not termed law (*fiqh*) in technical usage.

وقولنـا: «علـى التفصيل» فـي الأحكام وفي أدلّتها: تحـرّزًا من أصول الفقـه، فإنّ الفقيـه يعـرف آحاد مسـائل الأحكام، ويسـتدلّ بآحاد أدلّة، والأصوليّ إنّما يعرف أنواع الأحكام ويستدلّ عليها بآحاد الأدلّة من تعيين آحادهـا، وتحـرّزًا أيضًـا بقولنا: «علـى التفصيل» في الأدلّة من اسـتدلال المقلّد على الجملة، فإنّه يستدلّ بأصل إمامه على صحّة قوله.

Our statement "according to the detailed exposition in rulings and in their evidences" is to guard against legal theory (*uṣūl al-fiqh*), for the jurist (*faqīh*) knows individual instances of rulings and adduces individual evidences, whereas the legal theorist (*uṣūlī*) knows the kinds of rulings and adduces for them types of evidences without specifying their individual instances.

And it is also a safeguard – by our statement "in detail in the evidences" – against the inference of the imitator (*muqallid*) in general, for he infers from the foundational position of his Imām the soundness of his statement.

وأمّا أصول الفقه: فهو «العلـم بالأحكام الشـرعيّة الفرعيّة على الجملة وبأدواتها والاجتهاد فيها وما يتعلّق به».

Legal theory (*uṣūl al-fiqh*) is the knowledge of the subsidiary legal rulings of the Sharīʿah in general, and of its instruments, of independent reasoning therein, and of what pertains to it."

---

5 See §5.4.

0.2   ON THE RATIONALE FOR DIVIDING THIS BOOK INTO THE FIVE AFOREMENTIONED ARTS

الفصل الثاني: في وجه تقسيم هذا الكتاب إلى الفنون الخمسة المذكورة

وذلك أنّ المقصود الأوّل إنّما هو معرفة الأحكام الشرعيّة، فهذا الفنّ هو المطلوب لنفسه، وإنّما احتيج إلى سائر الفنون من أجله، ولمّا كان ثبوت الأحكام متوقّفًا على الأدلّة احتيج إلى فنّ الأدلّة، ولمّا كان استنباط الأحكام من الأدلّة متوقّفًا على شروط الاجتهاد احتيج إلى فنّ في الأدلّة وشروطه، وكيفيّته من الترجيح وغيره، ثمّ إن ذلك كلّه يتوقّف على أدوات يحتاج إليها في فهمه والتصرّف فيه، وهي له آلات، وهي على نوعين: منها ما يرجع إلى المعاني وهو من المعارف العقليّة، ومنها ما يرجع إلى الألفاظ وهي فنّ المعارف اللغويّة، فانقسم العلم بالضرورة إلى تلك الفنون الخمسة، فقسمنا كتابَنا هذا إليها، وقدّمنا الأدوات، لأنّه لا يتوصّل إلى فهم ما سواها إلّا بعد فهمها.

The primary objective is the knowledge of the legal rulings (*aḥkām shar'iyyah*); thus, this art is sought for its own sake, and the need for the other arts arises only on its account.

Since the establishment (*thubūt*) of the rulings depends upon the evidences, there is a need for the art of evidences. And since deriving the rulings from the evidences depends upon the conditions of independent juristic reasoning (*ijtihād*), there is a need for an art concerning the evidences, its conditions, and the manner thereof – such as preferential weighing (*tarjīḥ*) and other matters.

All of that, in turn, depends upon instruments required for its comprehension and application. These are its tools, and they are of two kinds: those pertaining to meanings – which belongs to the art of intellectual cognitions; and those pertaining to expressions – which it is the art of linguistic cognitions.

Thus, the science necessarily divides into those five arts, and we have divided this book of ours accordingly. We have placed the instruments first, because nothing else can be understood without first understanding them.

1

ON INTELLECTUAL COGNITIONS

الفنّ الأوّل من علم الأصول في المعارف العقليّة

وفيه عشرة أبواب:

It comprises ten sections:

<table>
<tr><td>1.1</td><td>ON THE SOURCES OF KNOWLEDGE</td><td dir="rtl">الباب الأوّل: في مدارك العلوم</td></tr>
</table>

وهو ضربان: تصوّر وتصديق:

It is of two kinds: conception and assent.

فأمّا التصوّر، فإدراك الذوات المفردة كمعرفة معنى الجسم، والحركة، والحيوان، والجماد، والحادث، والقديم، وغير ذلك.

Conception (taṣawwur) is the apprehension of individual essences (*dhawāt*), such as the knowledge of the meaning of body, motion, animal, inanimate object, originated, pre-eternal, and the like.

وأمّا التصديق، فهو إسناد أمر إلى ذات بالنفي والإثبات، كقولنا: «الجسم حادث» و «الجسم ليس بقديم»، فالتصوّر مقدّم والتصديق متأخّر عنه.

Assent (taṣdīq) is the ascription of a matter to an essence by affirmation or negation, as in our saying: "The body is originated," and "The body is not pre-eternal." Thus, conception is prior, and assent is posterior to it.

ثمّ إنّ الإسناد التصديقيّ على خمسة أنواع: علم، وجهل، وشكّ، وظنّ، ووهم.

فالعلم: هو الجزم المطابق للحقّ، وقيل في حدّه: معرفة المعلوم على ما هو به، فاعترض بلزوم الدور، فقيل فيه العلم صفة توجب تمييزًا لا يحتمل النقيض.

والجهل: هو الجزم غير المطابق، وقد يقال فيه جهل مركّب.

والشكّ: هو احتمال أمرين فأكثر من غير ترجيح.

والظنّ: هو الاحتمال الراجح.

والوهم: هو الاحتمال المرجوح.

Assentual ascription is of five types: knowledge, ignorance, doubt, presumption, and delusion.

Knowledge (*ʿilm*) is definitive judgement corresponding to truth. It has also been defined as: apprehending the known as it is in itself. An objection was raised that this necessitates circularity, so it was said: knowledge is a quality that necessitates a discrimination not admitting of contradiction.

Ignorance (*jahl*) is non-correspondent definitive judgement, and it may be referred to as compound ignorance (*jahl murakkab*).

Doubt (*shakk*) is the possibility of two or more matters without preferential weighing (*tarjīh*).

Presumption (*ẓann*) is the preponderant supposition.

Delusion (*wahm*) is the less-preponderant supposition.

 تكميل

حكم العقل بأمر على أمر يُسمّى تصديقًا، فإن تكلّم به فهو خبر فإن رام الاحتجاج عليه سُمّي دعوى، فإن ذكره في معرض الحجّة سُمّي قضيّة.

The judgement of the intellect by ascribing one matter to another is called assent (*taṣdīq*). If it is expressed in speech, it is called a report (*khabar*); if one seeks to argue upon it, it is called a claim (*daʿwā*); and if it is mentioned in the course of an argument, it is called a proposition (*qaḍiyyah*).

<table>
<tr><td>1.2   ON THAT WHICH LEADS TO CONCEPTION</td><td style="text-align:right">الباب الثاني: فيما يوصل إلى التصوّر</td></tr>
</table>

وذلك ثلاثة أشياء: الحدّ، والرسم، واللفظ المرادف.

These are three things: the true definition, the descriptive definition, and the synonymous term.

فأمّا الحدّ: فهو تعريف ماهيّة الشيء بجنسه وفصله.

وأمّا الرسم: فهو تعريف ماهيّة الشيء بجنسه وخاصّته.

True definition (*ḥadd*) is the specification of the quiddity (*māhiyyah*) of a thing by its genus and its differentia.

Descriptive definition (*rasm*) is the specification of the quiddity of a thing by its genus and its proprium.

فقولنا: «ماهيّة الشيء»، هي التي يسأل عنها بـ «ما»، وتحرّزنا بذلك ممّا يسأل عنه بـ «أي» وبـ «أين» و «متى» و «كيف».

Our statement "the quiddity of a thing" refers to that which is inquired about with "what" (*mā*), and by this we guard against that which is inquired about with "which" (*ayy*), "where" (*ayna*), "when" (*matā*), and "how" (*kayfa*).

وقولنا: «بجنسه»، يشمل الجنس الأعلى وما تحته النوع، فإنّ النوع جنس بالنسبة إلى ما تحته، ولكن الأولى أن يذكر في الحدّ والرسم الجنس الأقرب.

Our statement "by its genus" includes the highest genus and that beneath it, namely the species (*nawʿ*), for the species is a genus in relation to what is beneath it. However, it is preferable that in the true definition and the descriptive definition the proximate genus be mentioned.

وقولنا في حدّ الحدّ «بفصله» هو الوصف اللازم الذاتيّ الذي لا يفهم الشيء بدون فهمه كالنطق النفسانيّ للإنسان.

Our statement in the true definition of true definition "by its differentia (*bi-faṣlihi*)" is the essential necessary attribute without the understanding of which the thing is not understood, such as mental speech (*nuṭq nafsānī*) for the human being.

وقولنا في حدّ الرسم «بخاصّته الخاصّة» وصف لازم، إلّا أنّه غير ذاتيّ فلا يتوقّف الفهم عليه كـ «الضحك بالقوّة» للإنسان، بقولنا «الإنسان هو الحيوان الناطق» حدّ، وقولنا: «الإنسان هو الحيوان الضاحك» رسم، وإنّما اشترطنا ذكر الجنس ليعمّ فيكون الحدّ والرسم جامعًا، وهو المقصود.

Our statement in the true definition of descriptive definition: "by its proprium (*khāṣṣah*)" is a concomitant attribute, except that it is not essential, so understanding does not depend upon it – such as potential laughter for the human being. When we say, "The human is the rational animal," that is a true definition. And when we say, "The human is the laughing animal," that is a descriptive definition (*rasm*).

We stipulated the mention of the genus (*jins*) so that the true definition and the descriptive definition may be comprehensive, and this is the intended purpose.

واشترطنا الفصل والخاصّة ليخرج غير المطلوب، فإنّهما وصفان يتميّز بهما الموصوف من غيره فيكون الحدّ أو الرسم مانعًا وهو المنعكس، وقد يسقط ذكر الجنس من الحدّ أو الرسم فيكون ناقصًا كقولنا: «الإنسان هو الناطق» أو «الضاحك».

NOTE

We stipulated the differentia (*faṣl*) and the proprium (*khāṣṣah*) in order to exclude what is not intended, for they are two attributes by which the described is distinguished from what is other than it, so that the true definition or the descriptive definition is exclusive – that is, reciprocal.

The mention of the genus (*jins*) may be omitted from the true definition or the descriptive definition, rendering it deficient (*nāqiṣ*), as in our saying: "The human is the rational," or, "The human is the laughing."

وأمّا اللفظ المرادف فنحو قولنا: «البر» وتقول: «القمـح»، ويشترط أن يكون مسـاويًا لا أعمّ ولا أخصّ، ويحترز في الحـدّ والرسـم والمرادف من التعريف [بالمساوي]، والأخفى من الإجمال في اللفظ، ومن الدور، وهو التعريف بما لا يعرف إلّا بحدّ معرفة المطلوب، فيتوقّف.

Synonymous term (*lafẓ murādif*) is like our saying *burr* and your saying *qamḥ* [two words for wheat]. It is required that it be equal – neither more general nor more specific.

One must be cautious in the true definition, the descriptive definition, and the synonym against: defining by the equivalent (*musāwī*); defining by what is more obscure (*akhfā*); ambiguity (*ijmāl*) in the term; and *circularity* (*dawr*) – which is defining by that which is not known except through the definition of the thing sought, which results in a suspension.

NOTEتنبيه

الحـدّ غير المـحـدود إن أريد به اللفظ وهو نفسه، إن أريد به المعنى، فإنّ لكلّ شيء في الوجود أربع مراتب: حقيقتُه في نفسه، ومثالُه في الذهن، وذكرُه باللسان، وكتابتُه بالقلم.

The definition is other than the defined if by it is meant the term, and is itself if by it is meant the meaning. For every thing in existence has four levels: its reality in itself, its exemplar in the mind, its mention by the tongue, and its writing by the pen.

<table>
<tr><td>

1.3   ON THAT WHICH LEADS TO ASSENT

ON WHAT LEADS TO KNOWLEDGE
</td><td>

الباب الثالث: فيما يوصل إلى التصديق
</td></tr>
</table>

فالمُوصل إلى العلم يُسـمّى دليلًا، والمُوصل إلى الظنّ يُسـمّى أمارة، ثمّ إنّ الدليل ينقسم أربعة أنواع: سَمعيّ، وعقليّ، وحسّيّ، ومركّب من العقل والحسّ.

That which leads to knowledge is called a *proof* (*dalīl*), and that which leads to presumption is called a *sign* (*amārah*).

Then, the proof is divided into four types: auditory, intellectual, sensory, and composite of intellect and sense.

فأمّا السـمعيّ: فهو دليل الكتاب والسنّة المتواترة، والإجماع لا غير، فإنّ غيرها كالقياس وشبهه إنّما يفيد الظنّ.

Auditory proof (*samʿī*) is the proof from the Book, the recurrently mass-transmitted Sunnah (*sunnah mutawātirah*), and consensus (*ijmāʿ*), and nothing else, for other sources – such as analogical reasoning (*qiyās*) and the like – yield only presumption.

وأمّا العقليّ: فينقسم قسمين: ضروريّ، ونظريّ.

فالضـروريّ: هو الـذي لا يفتقـر إلى نظر واسـتدلال، ويُسـمّى أيضًا البديهيّ، كعلم الإنسان بوجود نفسه، وعلمه بأنّ الاثنين أكثر من الواحد، وعلمه بأنّ المصنوع لا بدّ له من صانع، وشبه ذلك من الأوليّات.

والنظريّ خلافه: وهو الذي يفتقر إلى نظر واستدلال.

Intellectual proof (*ʿaqlī*) is divided into two categories: immediate, and speculative.

The *immediate* (*ḍarūrī*) is that which does not require speculation (*naẓar*) or inference. It is also called the self-evident (*badīhī*). It is such as a human being's knowledge of his own existence, his knowledge that two is more than one, his knowledge that a manufactured thing must have a maker, and the like among the primary principles (*awwaliyyāt*).

The *speculative* (*naẓarī*) is its opposite: it is that which requires speculation (*naẓar*) and inference.

وأمّا الحسّـيّ: فهو الإدراك بالحواسّ الخمس، وهي: السـمع والبصر والشم، والذوق، واللمس.

وينخرط في سلكها الوجدانيّات كعلم الإنسان بلذته وألَمِه.

Sensory proof (*ḥissī*) is perception by the five senses, which are: hearing, sight, smell, taste, and touch.

Included under this category are the experiential introspections (*wajdāniyyāt*), such as a person's knowledge of his own pleasure and pain.

وأمّا المركّب عنهما من الحسّ والعقل، فهو التواتر والتجريب والحدس، وزاد أبو المعالي وأبو حامد قرائن الأحوال، كصفرة الوجل وحمرة الخجل، فتلخّص من هذا أنّ المفيدات للعلم تسعة وهي: السمع، وضرورة العقل، والنظـر العقلـيّ، والحسّ، والوجدان، والتواتر والتجريب، والحدس، وقرائن الأحوال.

That which is a composite of sense and intellect is: recurrent mass-transmission (*tawātur*), experimentation (*tajrīb*), and intuition (*ḥads*).

Abū al-Maʿālī and Abū Ḥāmid added contextual indicators (*qarāʾin al-aḥwāl*), such as the pallor of fear and the redness of shame.

From this it is concluded that the sources yielding knowledge are nine, namely: hearing, the immediacy of the intellect, intellectual speculation, sense perception, experiential introspection, recurrent mass-transmission, experimentation, intuition, and circumstantial indicators.

ON WHAT YIELDS PRESUMPTION

ثـمّ دون هــذه المرتبـة مـا يفيـد الظنّ وهـي ثلاثة أشـياء: المشـهورات، والمقبولات، والوهميّات.

Beneath this rank are those that yield presumption, and they are three things: the well-knowns, the accepteds, and the delusives.

فأمّا المشــهورات: فهي ما اتّفق عليه الناس أو أكثرهم أو به الأفاضل منهــم مـن العوائد وغيرها، وقد يحكـم العقل بمقتضى ذلك أو لا يحكم به ولا يخالفه.

Well-knowns (*mashhūrāt*) are those upon which people, or most of them, or the virtuous among them, have agreed – whether from customary practices and the like. The intellect (*ʿaql*) may judge in accordance with them, or it may not judge by them, yet it does not oppose them.

وأمّا المقبولات: فهي ما يخبر به الثقة أو الثقات الذين لم يبلغوا مبلغ التواتر، ولكن تسكن النفس إليها.

Accepteds (*maqbūlāt*) are that which is reported by a trustworthy person, or trustworthy persons who have not reached the level of recurrent mass-transmission, yet the soul finds repose in them.

وأمّا الوهميّات: فهي ما يتخيل أنّه عقليّ وليس كذلك.

Delusives (*wahmiyyāt*) are what is imagined to be intellectual but is not so.

1.4 ON THE CATEGORIES OF TERMS

الباب الرابع: في أسماء الألفاظ

وهي: المشـترك، والمترادف، والمتواطي، والمشـكّك، والمتباين، ونبيّنها بتقسيم وهو: أنّ اللفظ ومعناه على أربعة أقسام:

الأوّل: أن يتّحد اللفظ ويتعدّد المعنى فهو المشترك كالعين.

الثانـي: أن يتعدّد اللفظ ويتّحـد المعنى، فهو المترادف كالقمح والبر والحِنطة.

الثالث: أن يتحدّد اللفظ والمعنى، فإن كان معناه مسـتويًا في محاله كالرجل فهو المتواطي، وإن كان معناه متفاوتًا أو مختلفًا، فهو المشكّك كإطلاق النور على ضوء الشمس وضوء المصباح.

الرابـع: أن يتعـدّد اللفـظ والمعنـى، فهـو المتباين كالإنسـان والفرس والطير. ومن هذا التقسيم، تؤخذ حدودها.

They are: the equivocal, the synonymous, the univocal, the gradational, and the disparate.

We shall clarify them by means of a division, namely that the term and its meaning fall under four categories:

First: That the term be one while the meaning is multiple – this is the *equivocal* (*mushtarak*), such as *ʿayn*.[6]

Second: That the terms be multiple while the meaning is one – this is the *synonymous* (*mutarādif*), such as *qamḥ, burr,* and *ḥinṭah*.[7]

Third: That both the term and the meaning be one.

If its meaning is equal across its instances – such as "man" – then it is the *univocal* (*mutawāṭiʾ*).

---

6   (Tr:) The Arabic word *ʿayn* is the standard example of an equivocal term. Among its many meanings are: the eye, a spring of water, gold, a spy, and the essence of a thing.

7   All three – *qamḥ, burr,* and *ḥinṭah* – are Arabic names for wheat.

If its meaning is graded or varied, then it is the *gradational* (*mushakkik*), as in the application of "light" to the light of the sun and the light of a lamp.

Fourth: That both the term and the meaning be multiple – this is the *disparate* (*mutabāyin*), such as the human, the horse, and the bird.

Their definitions are taken from this division.

TWO NOTES   تنبيهان

الأوّل: قد يتوهّم في ألفاظ أنّها مترادفة، وهي متباينة كالسيف، والصارم، والمُهَنَّدِ، فإنّ السيف اسم للذات فقط والصارم باعتبار القطع، والمهنّد باعتبار أنّه من الهند. وكذلك قولنا «زيد متكلّم فصيح»، فإنّ الأوّل للذات، والثاني للصفة، والثالث لصفة الصفة.

First: It may be supposed that certain terms are synonymous, while in fact they are disparate – such as *sayf* (sword), *ṣārim* (cutter), and *muhannad* (Indian-forged). For *sayf* refers solely to the essence (*dhāt*), *ṣārim* refers in view of cutting, and *muhannad* refers in view of its being from India.

Likewise, when we say *Zayd mutakallim faṣīḥ*, the first [*Zayd*] refers to the essence, the second [*mutakallim*] to the attribute, and the third [*faṣīḥ*] to the attribute of the attribute.

الثاني: إنّ المشترك هو: اللفظ الموضوع لمعنيين وضعًا لم ينقل من أحدهما إلى الآخر، فإن كان منقولًا من أحدهما إلى الآخر فلا يُسمّى مشتركًا في الاصطلاح، ولكن إن نُقل لغير علاقة، سُمّي بالمنقول، وإن نُقل لعلاقة، سُمّي بالنظر إلى المعنى الأوّل حقيقةً وبالنظر إلى الثاني مجازًا.

Second: The equivocal (*mushtarak*) is the term assigned to two meanings by convention, without being transferred from one of them

to the other. If it is transferred from one to the other, it is not called
equivocal in technical usage: if transferred without a relation, it is the
transferred (*manqūl*); and if transferred with a relation, then with
respect to the first meaning it is literal (*ḥaqīqah*), and with respect
to the second it is figurative (*majāz*).

1.5 ON INDICATIONS   الباب الخامس: في الدَّلالة

وهي ثلاثة أنواع: مطابقة، وتضمّن، والتزام.

فدلالــة المطابقــة: هــي دلالة اللفظ على كمال مُسـمّاه كدلالة لفظ
البيت على جميعه.

ودلالة التضمّن: هي دلالة اللفظ على جزء مُسمّاه كدلالة لفظ البيت
على سقفه.

ودلالة التزام: هي دلالة اللفظ على لازم مُسمّاه كدلالة السقف على
الجدار.

They are three types: accordance, inclusion, and necessary entailment.

Indication by accordance (*dalālat al-muṭābaqah*) is the indication
of a term for the entirety of its referent, such as the indication of the
term "house" for all of it.

Indication by inclusion (*dalālat al-taḍammun*) is the indication
of a term for a part of its referent, such as the indication of the term
"house" for its roof.

Indication by necessary entailment (*dalālat al-iltizām*) is the
indication of a term for what is entailed by its referent, such as the
indication of the roof for the wall.

 تنبيهات ثلاثة

الأوّل: زاد فخـر الديـن بن الخطيب قيدًا فـي دلالة التضمّن وهو أن قال على جزء مُسـمّاه من حيـث هو جزء تحرز من دلالـة اللفظة بالمطابقة على معنى، وبالتضمّن على غيره كقولنا: «حرف» لأحد حروف المعنى نحـو: لَيْـتَ، ولَعَلَّ وحرف اللام وحدها بمعنى حرف هجاء، فالأوّل يدلّ على اللام بالتضمّن، والثاني يدلّ عليها مطابقةً.

First: Fakhr al-Dīn ibn al-Khaṭīb added a qualification to indication by inclusion, namely his statement: "of a part of its referent insofar as it is a part." This safeguards against a word indicating one meaning by accordance and another by inclusion, such as our saying *ḥarf* for one of the particles of meaning, like *layta* and *laʿalla*, and our saying "the particle *lām*" alone, meaning a letter of the alphabet. The first indicates *lām* by inclusion, while the second indicates it by accordance.

الثاني: يشترط في دلالة الالتزام أن تكون الملازمة في الذهن والخارج، أو في الذهن خاصّةً لا في الخارج خاصّةً.

Second: For indication by necessary entailment to obtain, it is required that the concomitance be either in both the mind (*dhihn*) and external ontological actuality (*khārij*), or in the mind alone – not in external ontological actuality alone.

الثالث: جعل شهاب الدين القرافيّ الدلالة قسمين: دلالة اللفظ وهي ما ذكرنا، والدلالة باللفظ: وهي اسـتعمال المتكلّم اللفظ في حقيقته أو مجازه.

Third: Shihāb al-Dīn al-Qarāfī classified indication (*dalālah*) into two categories: the indication *of* the term, which is what we have mentioned; and the indication *by* the term, which is the speaker's use of the term in its literal or figurative sense.

1.6 ON THE DISTINCTION BETWEEN THE PARTICULAR AND THE UNIVERSAL, THE WHOLE AND THE PART, AND UNIVERSALITY AND PARTICULARITY

الباب السادس: في الفرق بين الجزئيّ والكلّيّ، والكلّ والجزء والكلّيّة والجزئيّة

أمّـا الكلّـيُّ: فهو الـذي لا يمنع تصوّر معنـاه من تعدّده سـواء وجد في الوجود متعدّدًا كالإنسان أو واحدًا كالشمس أو لم يوجد في الوجود، فإنّ الاعتبار هنا من جهة تصوّره في الذهن.

Universal (*kullī*) is that whose conception does not prevent the multiplicity of its instances, whether it exists (1) in external ontological actuality (*wujūd ʿaynī*) (a) as multiple, such as "human," or (b) as singular, such as "the sun," or (2) whether it does not exist in external ontological actuality at all – for the consideration here pertains to its conception in the mind.

أمّا الجزئيّ: فهو الذي يدلّ على واحد بعينه كالاسم العلم.

Particular (*juzʾī*) is that which signifies one specific individual, such as a proper name (*ʿalam*).

ويسـمّي النحويّـون الكلّـيّ نكـرةً، ويسـمّون الجزئـيّ معرفةً، وأنواعها خمسـة: المضمر: وأسـماء الإشـارة، والعلم، والمعرّف بالألف واللام، والمضاف إلى المعرفة.

The grammarians refer to the universal as *indefinite* (*nakirah*), and they refer to the particular as *definite* (*maʿrifah*).

Its types [i.e. of the definite] are five: the pronoun, the demonstrative nouns, the proper name, the noun made definite by the definite article, and the noun annexed to a definite noun.

فائدة

المضمـر عنـد أكثـر الناس جزئـيّ كاختصاصـه بمتكلّـم أو مخاطب أو غائب، وقال النحويّون فيه: إنّه أعرف المعارف.

وقال شهاب الدين: إنّه كلّيّ في وضعه وإنّما اختصّ في استعماله.

The pronoun (*muḍmar*), according to most people, is a particular, by virtue of its being restricted to a speaker, or an addressee, or an absent one. The grammarians have said concerning it that it is the most definite of the definites (*maʿrifah*).

Shihāb al-Dīn said: it is universal in designation, but particular in usage.

وأمّا الكلّ: فهو المجموع بجملته كأسماء الأعداد.

والجزء: هو ما تركّب الكلّ منه كتركيب العشرة من اثنين في خمسة.

Whole (*kull*) is the totality in its entirety, such as the names of numbers.

Part (*juzʾ*) is that of which the whole is composed, as ten is composed of two times five.

وأمّا الكلّيّـة: فهي ما يقتضي الحكم على كلّ فرد من أفراد الحقيقة، كقوله تعالى: ﴿كُلُّ مَنْ عَلَيْهَا فَانٍ﴾ [الرحمن ٢٦].

والجزئيّة: ما تقتضي الحكم على بعض أفراد الحقيقة، كقولنا: «بعض الحيوان إنسان».

Universality (*kulliyyah*) is that which entails judgement upon every individual of the reality, as in His saying, exalted is He: "Everyone upon it is perishing."[8]

---

8   Qurʾān, 55:26.

Particularity (*juz'iyyah*) is that which entails judgement concerning some individuals of the quiddity, as in our saying: "Some animal is a human."

<table>
<tr><td>CLARIFICATION</td><td>بيان</td></tr>
</table>

قد يعسر الفرق بين الكلّ والكلّيّة، وهو أنّ الحكم في الكلّ على المجموع لا على كلّ فرد بانفراده، وذلك كقولنا: «كلّ إنسان يَشِيلُ الصخرة العظيمة»، والحكم في الكلّيّة على كلّ فرد بانفراده حتى لا يبقى فرد، كقولنا: «كلّ إنسان يشبعه رغيف».

It may be difficult to differentiate between the whole (*kull*) and the universality (*kulliyyah*).

The judgement with respect to the whole is upon the aggregate, not upon each individual separately, as in our saying: "Every human lifts the great rock."

The judgement with respect to universality, on the other hand, is upon each individual separately, such that no individual is excluded, as in our saying: "Every human is satiated by a loaf of bread."

<table>
<tr><td>1.7   ON THE RELATION OF ONE REALITY OF ANOTHER]</td><td>الباب السابع: في نسبة بعض الحقيقة من بعض</td></tr>
</table>

إذا نظرنا إلى حقيقة مع أخرى وجدتها على أربعة أقسام:

If we consider one quiddity in relation to another, we find it to fall under four categories:

الأوّل: أن تكون إحداهما أعمّ مطلقًا، والأخرى أخصّ مطلقًا، كالحيوان والإنسان، يستدلّ بوجود الأخصّ على وجود الأعمّ، وينفي الأعمّ على نفي الأخصّ، ولا دليل في عدم الأخصّ ولا في وجود الأعمّ.

First: That one of them is absolutely more general, and the other is absolutely more specific, such as "animal" and "human." The existence of the more specific is evidence for the existence of the more general, and the negation of the more general is evidence for the negation of the more specific. There is no inference from the nonexistence of the more specific, nor from the existence of the more general.

الثاني: أن يكون كلّ واحد منهما أعمّ من وجه وأخصّ من وجه آخر كالإنسان والأبيض، فلا دليل لأحدهما على الآخر أصلًا.

Second: That each of the two is more general in one respect and more specific in another, such as "human" and "white"; thus, neither serves as any proof for the other whatsoever.

الثالث: أن يكونا متساويين كالإنسان والضاحك بالقوّة، فيستدلّ بوجود كلّ واحد منهما على وجود الآخر، وبعدمه على عدمه.

Third: That the two are equivalent (*mutasāwiyān*[9]), such as "human" and "the one potentially laughing," so that the existence of each of them is inferred from the existence of the other, and its nonexistence from the nonexistence of the other.

الرابع: أن يكونا متباينين كالحيوان والجماد.

Fourth: That the two are disparate (*mutabāyinān*), such as "animal" and "inanimate object."

والمعلومات أيضًا على ثلاثة أقسام:

١. نقيضان: وهما اللذان لا يجتمعان معًا ولا يرتفعان معًا كوجود زيد وعدمه، فيستدلّ بوجود أحدهما على عدم الآخر، وبعدمه على وجوده.

---

9   (Tr:) i.e. coextensive: their extensions are identical. Every instance of one is an instance of the other.

٢. وضدّان: وهما اللذان لا يجتمعان ويمكن ارتفاعهما كالسواد والبياض، فيستدلّ بوجود أحدهما على عدم الآخر، ولا دليل في عدم واحد منهما.

٣. وخلافان: وهما اللذان يمكن اجتماعهما وارتفاعهما كالإنسان والفرس، فلا دليل في وجود واحد منهما ولا في عدمه.

Objects of knowledge (*maʿlūmāt*) are also divided into three categories:

1. *Contradictories* (*naqīḍān*) – they are those that neither coexist nor are both absent, such as the existence of Zayd and his non-existence. The existence of one is evidence for the nonexistence of the other, and its nonexistence is evidence for the existence of the other.

2. *Contraries* (*ḍiddān*) – they are those that cannot coexist, yet may both be absent, such as "blackness" and "whiteness." The existence of one is evidence for the nonexistence of the other, but the nonexistence of one is not evidence for the other.

3. *Differents* (*khilāfān*) – they are those that may both coexist and may both be absent, such as "human" and "horse." Thus, there is no evidence in the existence of either of them, nor in their nonexistence.

قانون في هذا الباب: وذلك بإدخال «كلّ» على إحدى الحقيقتين والإخبار بالأخرى فإن صدقت القضيّة من الجهتين فهما متساويان كقولنا: «كلّ إنسان ضاحك، وكلّ ضاحك إنسان»، وإن كذبت من الجهتين، فهما متباينان، أو أعمّ من وجه وأخصّ من وجه، وإن صدقت من الجهة الواحدة، فهما أعمّ مطلقًا وأخصّ مطلقًا كقولك: «كلّ إنسان حيوان»، والمضاف إلى «كلُّ» هو الأخصّ، والخبر هو الأعمّ، وإن عكستها كذبت.

A law relevant to this discussion is by applying "every" to one of the two quiddities (*ḥaqīqah*) and predicating the other of it.

If the proposition is true in both directions, then the two are equivalent (*mutasāwiyān*), as in our saying: "Every human is a laughing one, and every laughing one is a human."

If it is false in both directions, then the two are either disparate (*mutabāyinān*), or one is more general in one respect and more specific in another.

If it is true in one direction only, then the two are absolutely more general and absolutely more specific, as in our saying: "Every human is an animal." That which is annexed to "every" is the more specific, and the predicate is the more general. If you reverse it, it becomes false.

<table>
<tr><td>1.8</td><td>ON THE TYPES OF
INTELLECTUAL ARGUMENTS</td><td dir="rtl">الباب الثامن: في أنواع
الحجج العقليّة</td></tr>
</table>

وهي ثلاثة أنواع: قياس، واستقراء، وتمثيل.

They are three types: syllogism, induction, and analogy.

فأمّا القياس: فهو عبارة عن كلام مُؤلَّفٍ مقدِمتين فأكثر، يتولد منهما نتيجة وهي المطلوب إثباتها أو نفيها، فنذكره في موضعه.

وهـذا القيـاس في اصـطلاح أهل المنطق، وأمّا القيـاس في اصطلاح الفقهـاء فنذكـره فـي موضعـه. ثـمّ إنّ هذا القيـاس المنطقـيّ إن كانت مقدّماته قطعيّةً وركّبت كما يجب بشروطها، سُمّي برهان، وكانت النتيجة علمًا يقينيًّا، وإن كانت مقدّماته أو واحدة منهما غير قطعيّة أو دخله خلل فـي التركيـب أو نقص من شـروطها لم يفد اليقيـن، وقد يفيد الظنّ أو ما دونه.

Syllogism (*qiyās*) is speech composed of two premises or more, from which a conclusion (*natījah*) is generated, which is what is sought (*maṭlūb*), whether to be affirmed or negated. And we shall mention it in its proper place.[10]

This is the syllogism (*qiyās*) in the terminology of the logicians.

The syllogism in the terminology of the jurists we shall mention it in its proper place.[11]

Then, this logical syllogism – if its premises are certain and it is composed as it ought with its conditions – then it is called a *demonstration* (*burhān*), and the conclusion is certain knowledge (*'ilm yaqīnī*). But if its premises, or one of them, are not certain, or if a flaw enters into the composition, or a condition is lacking, then it does not yield certain knowledge; rather, it may yield presumption (*ẓann*) or something less than that.

وأمّا الاستقراء: فهو أن ينظر الحكم في كثير من أفراد الحقيقة، فيوجد فيها على حالة واحدة، فيغلب على الظنّ أنّه على تلك الحالة في جميع أفراد الحقيقة .

Induction (*istiqrā'*) is to examine the judgement in many instances of the quiddity and find it in them in one state, so that the preponderant presumption becomes that it is in that state in all instances of the quiddity.

وأمّا التمثيل: فهو أن يحكم لجزء بحكم جزء آخر وهو أضعفها .

Analogy (*tamthīl*) is to judge for one part with the judgement of another part, and it is the weakest of them.

والفـرق بينهـا: أنّ القياس احتجاج منقول علـى معنى كلّيّ إلى معنى كلّيّ تحته، أو إلى جزئيّ، وأن الاسـتقراء منقول من جزئيّات متعدّدة إلى كلّيّ، وأن التمثيل منقول من جزئيّ إلى جزئيّ .

---

10 See §1.9.

11 See §4.7.

The distinction between them is that syllogism is an argument carried from a universal meaning to a universal subsumed under it, or to a particular; induction is an argument carried from multiple particulars to a universal; and analogy is an argument carried from a particular to a particular.

<table>
<tr><td>1.9   ON THE TYPES OF
LOGICAL SYLLOGISM</td><td align="right">الباب التاسع: في أنواع القياس
المنطقيّ</td></tr>
</table>

وهو خمسة: برهان، وجدل، وخطابة، وشعر، وسفسطة.

They are five: demonstration, dialectical reasoning, rhetoric, poetry, and sophistry.

فأمّا البرهان: فهو القياس اليقينيّ الصحيح.

الصحيح: وهو الذي تكون مقدّماته قطعيّةً كلّها البديهيّات، والنظريّات الصحيحة، والحسّيّة السالمة من غلط الحسّ.

Demonstration (*burhān*) is the certain, sound syllogism.

The sound [syllogism] is: that whose premises are all definitive – namely, the self-evident (*badīhiyyāt*), the correct speculatives (*naẓariyyāt*), and the sensibles (*ḥissiyyāt*) free from error of sense.

وأمّا الجدل: فهو الذي تكون مقدّماته مقبولةً أو مشـهورةً عند الكافة وهي في الأغلب صادقة، وقد تكون كاذبةً في النادر.

وفائدة الجدل أن يغلب الخصم خصمه.

Dialectical reasoning (*jadal*) is that whose premises are the accepteds (*maqbūlāt*) or the well-knowns (*mashhūrāt*) among the masses. They are mostly true, though in rare cases they may be false.

The benefit of dialectical reasoning is that one disputant prevails over his opponent.

وأمّا الخطابة: فهي التي تكون مقدّماتها مقبولةً يحصل بها غلبة الظنّ فتقتنـع النفـس بها وتركن إليهـا مع حضور نقيضها بالبال، أو قبول النفس لنقيضها.

وفائدة الخطابة أن يميل السامع إلى ما يراد منه ويركن إليه ويقوي ذلك بفصاحة الكلام وعذوبة الألفاظ وطيب النغمة.

Rhetoric (khiṭābah) is that whose premises are the accepteds (*maqbūlāt*), yielding predominance of presumption, so that the soul is persuaded by them and inclines to them, even with their contradictory present to mind, or with the soul's acceptance of their contradictory.

The benefit of rhetoric is that the listener inclines toward what is intended of him and leans to it, and this is reinforced by the eloquence of speech, the sweetness of expressions, and the pleasantness of tone.

وأمّا الشـعر: فهو ما يتضمّن تشـبيهًا أو تمثيلًا أو اسـتعارةً، أو تخييل أمر في النفس يقصد به الترغيب أو الترهيب أو التشـجيع أو الحثّ على العطـاء أو تحريـك فـرح أو حزن أو تقريب بعيد أو غير ذلك، وهو يؤثّر في النفس مع العلم بكذبه، ويشتمل تأثيره بحسن الصوت والتلحين.

Poetry (shiʿr) is that which contains a simile (*tashbīh*), or an analogy (*tamthīl*), or a metaphor (*istiʿārah*), or the imaginative depiction (*takhyīl*) of something within the soul, intended for instilling desire or fear, or for encouragement, or for urging generosity, or for stirring joy or sorrow, or for rendering the distant near, or other such aims.

It affects the soul even with knowledge of its falsehood, and its effect is strengthened by pleasant voice and melodic intonation.

وأمّـا السفسـطة: فهـي المغالطـة، والغلط يقع بوجـوه كثيرة من جهة اللفظ أو من جهة المعنى أو من طريق الحذف والإضمار، أو في تركيب المقدّمات الوهميّة مكان القطعيّة إلى غير ذلك.

Sophistry (*safsaṭah*) is fallacy (*mughālaṭah*).

Fallacy occurs in many forms – either from the side of the term, or from the side of the meaning, or by way of elision and ellipsis, or in composing delusive premises in place of definitive ones, and so on.

تحقيــق هـذه الألفـاظ في هـذا الاصطلاح بخلاف معناهـا في اللغة والاصطلاح العامّ:

The precise determination of these terms in this technical usage differs from their meaning in language and in general usage:

أمّـا البرهـان: فهـو فـي اللغة كلّ مـا يوصل إلى التحقيق، سـواء كان كلامًا أو غيره.

وفـي هـذا الاصـطلاح كلام مُؤَلَّفٌ علـى وجـه مخصـوص بشـروط مخصوصة.

Demonstration (*burhān*), in language, is anything that leads to establishing the truth, whether it be speech or otherwise.

In this technical usage, it is a composition articulated in a specific manner with specific conditions.

وأمّا الخطابة فهي في اللغة كلام الخطيب سواء تكلّم بما يفيد الظنّ أو اليقين وهي هنا ما يفيد الظنّ خاصّةً.

Rhetoric (*khiṭābah*), in language, is the speech of the orator, whether he speaks with that which yields presumption or certainty. Here, it is that which yields presumption (*ẓann*), specifically.

وأمّا الشعر: فهو في هذا الاصطلاح أعمّ منه في الاصطلاح العامّ لأنّه هنا المجاز والتمثيل وشـبه ذلك، ممّا ليس بحقيقة سـواء كان منظومًا أو منثورًا، وهو في الاصطلاح العامّ: المنظوم الأعاريض المعروفة.

Poetry (*shiʿr*), in this technical usage, is broader than it is in general usage, for here it refers to the figurative (*majāz*), the analogy (*tamthīl*), and the like – anything that is not literal, whether metered or unmetered. In general usage, it is the metered composition upon the known prosodic patterns.

1.10   ON DEMONSTRATION

الباب العاشر: في البرهان

ونتكلّم في أجزائه التي تتركّب منها، وفي ضروبه.

We shall speak concerning its parts of which it is composed, and concerning its kinds.

[ITS PARTS]

أمّا أجزاؤه فلا بدّ في كلّ برهان وقياس منطقيّ من مقدّمتين فأكثر ونتيجة تحذف إحدى المقدّمتين للعلم بها.

As for its parts: Every demonstration (*burhān*) and logical syllogism (*qiyās manṭiqī*) must consist of two premises or more and a conclusion, with one of the premises sometimes omitted because it is already known.

والمقدّمة هي جملة خبريّة تُسمّى قضيّة، وتشتمل على موضوع ومحمول ويسمّي أهل المنطق المخبر عنه بالموضوع والخبر بالمحمول، ويسمّيها النحويّون مبتدأ وخبرًا، ويسمّي الفقهاء حكمًا، والمبتدأ محكومًا عليه.

A *premise* (*muqaddamah*) is a declarative sentence called a proposition (*qaḍiyyah*), and it comprises a subject and a predicate.

The logicians call the entity about which something is asserted the *subject* (*mawḍūʿ*), and the assertion itself the *predicate* (*maḥmūl*).

The grammarians call them the *subject* (*mubtadaʾ*) and the *predicate* (*khabar*).[12]

---

12   (Tr:) The Arabic terms used by the logicians (*mawḍūʿ* and *maḥmūl*) and the grammarians (*mubtadaʾ* and *khabar*) are entirely distinct; the author's point is that three disciplines employ different terminology for the same two

The jurists call the predicate the *ruling* (*ḥukm*), and the subject the *one upon whom the judgement is made* (*maḥkūm ʿalayh*).

ويشترط أن تكون ما تقتضيه هذه القضيّة من نفي أو إثبات معلومًا أو مُسَلَّمًا عند الخصم، فإذا ازدوجت هذه القضيّة وهي المقدّمة مع مثلها، تولّدت بينهما النتيجة، وهي جملة أخرى خبريّة تُسمّى أيضًا قضيّة، وهي التـي قصد إثباتهـا أو نفيها، ولذلك يقول الفقهاء وجـه الدليل ويعنون به وجه لزوم النتيجة من المقدّمات.

It is required that what this proposition entails – whether negation or affirmation – be known or conceded by the opponent. When this proposition, which is the premise (*muqaddamah*), is joined with another like it, a *conclusion* (*natījah*) is generated between them.

This conclusion is another declarative sentence, also called a *proposition* (*qadiyyah*), and it is that which was intended to be affirmed or negated. For this reason, the jurists say "the aspect of the proof" (*wajh al-dalīl*) by which they mean the aspect of the entailment of the consequent (*tālī*) from the premises (*muqaddamāt*).

[ITS KINDS]

وتنقسم القضايا أيضًا قسمين: موجبة وهي المثبتة، وسالبة وهي المنفية.

Propositions are also divided into two types: affirmative (*mūjibah*), which affirms; and negative (*sālibah*), which denies.

وتنقسـم كلّ واحـدة أربعة أقسـام: كلّيّة محصـورة، وجزئيّة محصورة، وشخصيّة، ومهملة.

Each of these is further divided into four categories: bounded universal, bounded particular, personal, and indefinite.

---

elements of a proposition. In English, both pairs naturally render as "subject" and "predicate," which obscures the contrast the Arabic makes self-evident.

والجزئيّة المحصورة نحو قولنا: «بعض الحيوان إنسان»، واللفظ الحاصر لهما يُسمّى سيورًا نحو «كلّ» و «بعض».

فالكلّيّة المحصورة هي التي يكون موضوعها عامًّا كقولنا: «كلّ مسكر حرام».

والشخصيّة: هي التي يكون موضوعها جزئيًّا كقولنا: «زيد قائم».

والمهملـة: وهـي التي يتبيّن فيها أنّ الحكـم للكلّ أو للبعض كقولنا: ﴿إِنَّ الْإِنْسَانَ لَفِي خُسْرٍ﴾ [العصر ٢].

The *bounded universal* (*kulliyyah maḥṣūrah*) is that whose subject is general, such as our saying: "Every intoxicant is forbidden."

The *bounded particular* (*juz'iyyah maḥṣūrah*)[13] is like our saying: "Some animals are human beings." The term that restricts both is called a quantifier (*sūr*), such as "every" and "some."

The *personal* (*shakhṣiyyah*) is that whose subject is particular, as in our saying: "Zayd is standing."

The *indefinite* (*muhmalah*) is that in which it is not evident whether the judgement pertains to the whole or to a part, as in His saying: "Indeed, man is in loss."[14]

إلّا أنّ الشـخصيّة والمهملة مطرحتان في العلوم، فبقيت المحصورتان الكلّيّـة والجزئيّـة، وكلّ واحدة منهما تكون موجبةً وسـالبةً، فالقضايا على هذا أربع.

However, the personal and the indefinite propositions are set aside in the sciences. What remains are the two bounded ones: the

---

13   (Tr:) A bounded or quantified (*maḥṣūrah*) proposition is one that contains an explicit quantifier (*sūr*) – such as "every" or "some" – that delimits whether the judgement applies to the whole or part of the subject. This is in contrast to the indefinite (*muhmalah*), which lacks such a quantifier.

14   Qur'ān, 103:2.

universal and the particular. Each of these may be affirmative or negative; thus the propositions, on this basis, are four.

[ITS KINDS]

ثمّ إنّ البرهان من طريق صورة تركيبه على ثلاثة أضرب:

Then, demonstration (*burhān*), in terms of the form of its composition, is of three kinds.

[1. THE CONNECTING SYLLOGISM]

الضرب الأوّل: ويسمّيه بعض الناس القياس الاقترانيّ، ويسمّيه أهل المنطق الحمليّ، ويسمّيه أهل اللغة برهان العلّة، وهو يشتمل على مقدّمتين، في كلّ مقدّمة محمول وموضوع وهما الحكم والمحكوم عليه فتلك أربعة أشياء، إلّا أن واحدًا منها يتكرّر في المقدّمتين فتبقى ثلاثة أشياء يسمّيها أهل المنطق حدودًا وهي الحدّ الأوسط، والحدّ الأكبر والحدّ الأصغر.

The First Kind [of Demonstration]: Some people call it the connecting syllogism (*qiyās iqtirānī*), the logicians call it the *predicative* (*ḥamlī*), and the linguists call it the *proof of the cause (burhān al-ʿillah)*.

It comprises two premises; each premise contains a predicate and a subject – namely, the judgement (*ḥukm*) and the one upon whom the judgement is made (*maḥkūm ʿalayh*). Thus, there are four elements, but one of them is repeated in both premises, leaving three elements. Logicians call these "terms" (*ḥudūd*): the middle term (*ḥadd awsaṭ*), the major term (*ḥadd akbar*), and the minor term (*ḥadd aṣghar*).

فأمّا الحدّ الأوسط فيسمّيه الفقهاء علّةً، وهو الذي يتكرّر في المقدّمتين.

وأمّا الحدّ الأكبر: فهو الحكم وهو الذي يكون في النتيجة محمولًا.

وأمّا الحدّ الأصغر: فهو المحكوم عليه وهو الذي يكون في النتيجة موضوعًا.

والمقدّمة التي فيها الأصغر تُسمّى صغرى.

والمقدّمة التي فيها الحدّ الأكبر تُسمّى كبرى.

The *middle term* (*ḥadd awsaṭ*) is what the jurists call the *cause* (*'illah*); it is that which recurs in both premises.

The *major term* (*ḥadd akbar*) is the *judgement* (*ḥukm*); and it is that which, in the conclusion, is the predicate (*maḥmūl*).

The *minor term* (*ḥadd aṣghar*) is the *one upon whom the judgement is made* (*maḥkūm 'alayh*); it is that which, in the conclusion, is the subject.

The premise in which the minor term (*ḥadd aṣghar*) appears is called the *minor premise* (*ṣughrā*).

The premise in which the major term (*ḥadd akbar*) appears is called the *major premise* (*kubrā*).

ومثـال ذلـك قولنا: «كلّ مسـكر حرام، والنبيذ مسـكر، فالنبيذ حرام»

فقولنا: «كلّ مسكر» كلّيّة موجبة وهي المقدّمة الكبرى.

وقولنـا: «النبيذ مسـكر» مقدّمـة أخرى، وهي أيضًـا كلّيّة موجبة وهي المقدّمة الصغرى.

وقولنا: «والنبيذ حرام» هي النتيجة.

والحدّ الأوسـط هو «المسكر» لأنّه تكرّر في المقدّمتين، والأصغر هو «النبيـذ» لأنّـه موضوع في النتيجة وهو المحكـوم عليه، والحدّ الأكبر هو «الحرام»، لأنّه محمول في النتيجة، وهو الحكم.

An example of this is our saying: "Every intoxicant is forbidden. *Nabīdh* is an intoxicant. Therefore, *nabīdh* is forbidden."

Our statement "Every intoxicant is forbidden" is a universal affirmative, and it is the major premise.

Our statement "*nabīdh* is an intoxicant" is another premise, and it is also a universal affirmative. It is the minor premise.

Our statement "*nabīdh* is forbidden" is the conclusion (*natījah*).

The middle term is "intoxicant," because it recurs in both premises.

The minor term is "*nabīdh*," because it is the subject in the conclusion and the one upon whom the judgement is passed.

The major term is "forbidden," because it is the predicate in the conclusion and it is the judgement (*ḥukm*).

ثمّ إنّ هذا الضرب له ثلاثة أشكال:

Then, this kind has three figures (*ashkāl*).[15]

الشكل الأوّل: أن يكون الحدّ الأوسط موضوعًا في إحدى المقدّمتين محمـولًا فـي الأخـرى، فإن عبّرت بعبارة الفقهاء، قلـتَ أن تكون العلّة حكمًـا فـي إحدى المقدّمتين محكومًا عليـه في الأخرى وذلك كالمثال الذي ذكرنا ألا ترى أنّ المسكر -وهو العلّة- وقع محكومًا عليه في قولنا: «كلّ مسكر حرام»، ووقع حكمًا في قولنا: «النبيذ مسكر».
ويشـترط في هذا المثال أن تكون المقدّمة الصغرى موجبة لا سـالبة، وأن تكون الكبرى كلّيّة لا جزئيّة، وحينئذٍ تنتج نتيجة صحيحة.

The First Figure: That the middle term be the subject in one of the premises and the predicate in the other.

If you were to express it in the terminology of the jurists, you would say: that the cause (*ʿillah*) be a judgement (*ḥukm*) in one of the premises and the one upon whom the judgement is made (*maḥkūm ʿalayh*) in the other.

This is like the example we mentioned. Do you not see that the intoxicant – which is the cause – occurs as the one upon whom the judgement is passed in our statement "Every intoxicant is forbidden," and occurs as a judgement in our statement "*Nabīdh* is an intoxicant."

It is stipulated in this figure that the minor premise be affirmative, not negative, and that the major premise be universal, not particular; in that case, a correct conclusion results.

---

15   (Tr:) Note that he is among those who omitted the fourth figure.

الشــكل الثانـي: أن يكــون الحدّ الأوسـط محمـولًا فـي المقدّمتين، ويسـمّيه الفقهاء «الفرق»، يشـترط في إنتاجه أن تكون الكبرى كلّيّةً، وأن تكون إحدى المقدّمتين مخالفةً للأخرى في الإيجاب والسلب.

ومثالـه قولنـا: «كلّ ثـوب مـزروع، ولا ربـويّ مـزروع، فلا ثـوب واحد ربويّ».

The Second Figure: That the middle term is the predicate in both premises; the jurists call it "differentiation" (*farq*).

For it to yield a conclusion, it is required that the major premise be universal, and that one of the two premises oppose the other by being affirmative and negative.

An example of this is our saying: "Every garment is cultivated. No usurious item is cultivated. Therefore, no garment is usurious."

الشــكل الثالـث: أن يكــون الحدّ الأوسـط موضوعًا فـي المقدّمتين، ويسـمّيه الفقهـاء بـ «النقـض»، ويشـترط في إنتاجـه أن تكـون المقدّمة الصغرى موجبةً وأن تكون إحداهما كلّيّةً.

ومثالـه قولنـا: «كلّ قمـح مطعـوم، وكلّ قمح ربويّ، فبعـض المطعوم ربويّ».

The Third Figure: That the middle term be the subject in both premises; the jurists call it "inversion" (*naqḍ*).

For it to yield a conclusion, it is required that the minor premise be affirmative, and that one of the two premises be universal.

An example of this is our saying: "Every wheat is edible, and every wheat is usurious. Therefore, some edible is usurious."[16]

---

16   (Tr:) The author omits the Fourth Figure. This is often done on the grounds that it is rare or of little use in the sciences.

THREE NOTES تنبيهات ثلاثة

الأوّل: متى كان في البرهان مقدّمة سالبة أو جزئيّة أو مظنونة كانت النتيجة كذلك، لأنّها تتبع أخسّ المقدّمات، ولا تتبع أشرفها.

First: Whenever a demonstration (*burhān*) contains a negative, a particular, or a conjectural premise, the conclusion will likewise be so, for the conclusion follows the lowest of the premises, not the highest.

الثاني: تجتمع الأشكال الثلاثة في أنّها لا تنتج إذا كانت المقدّمتان معًا سالبتين أو جزئيّتين.

Second: The three figures are alike in that they do not yield a conclusion if both premises are negative or both are particular.

الثالث: لا تكون نتيجة الشكل الثاني إلّا سالبةً، ولا تكون نتيجة الشكل الثالث إلّا جزئيّةً، أمّا نتيجة الشكل الأوّل فتكون موجبةً أو سالبةً، أو كلّيّةً أو جزئيّةً.

Third: The conclusion of the second figure is only negative, and the conclusion of the third figure is only particular

The conclusion of the first figure may be affirmative or negative, and universal or particular.

SUMMARY تلخيص

يتصوّر في تركيب كلّ شكل ستّ عشرة صورة، لأن كلّ واحد من المقدّمتين يمكن أن تكون على أربعة أنواع، وأربعة في أربعة ستّة عشر ولكن إنّما ينتج في الشكل الأوّل أربع صور، وفي الثاني أربع، وفي الثالث ستّ صور، ولا ينتج سائر الصور لعدم شروط الإنتاج فيها.

2. THE CONDITIONAL CONJOINING SYLLGOGISM

In the composition of each figure, sixteen configurations (*ṣuwar*) are conceivable, since each of the two premises may be of four kinds, and four times four is sixteen. However, only four configurations yield a conclusion in the first figure, four in the second, and six in the third. The remaining configurations do not yield a conclusion because the conditions for production are lacking in them.

[2. THE CONDITIONAL CONJOINING SYLLOGISM]

الضرب الثاني: الشرطيّ المتّصل، ويسمّيه الفقهـاء التلازم، وهو مركّب من مقدّمتين:

الأولى منهما مركّبة من قضيّتين، قرن إحداهما بحرف شرط، وتُسمّى المقدّمـة الأخـرى إجـزاء الشـرط، وتُسـمّى التالـي، وقد يُسـمّى المقدّم بالملزوم والتالي باللازم.

The Second Kind [of Demonstration]: The *conditional conjoining* (*sharṭī muttaṣil*), which the jurists call *concomitance* (*talāzum*). It is composed of two premises.

The first of them is composed of two propositions, one of which is joined with a conditional particle; the other proposition is called the *apodosis* (*ijzā' al-sharṭ*) and the *consequent* (*tālī*).

The antecedent may be referred to as the *concomitant antecedent* (*malzūm*), and the consequent as the *concomitant consequent* (*lāzim*).

المقدّمة الثانية من قضيّة واحدة قرن بها حرف استثناء على اصطلاح أهل المنطق مثل «لكن» أو لم يقرن، ويكون الكلام في معناه.

وتشـتمل هذه المقدّمة الثانية علـى ذكر إحدى القضيّتين المتقدّمتين تسليمًا إمّا بالنفي أو بالإثبات حتى ينتج إحدى القضيّتين أو نقيضها.

مثـال ذلــك: «إن كان الوتر يُؤَدِّي على الراحلة، فهو نافلة، ومعلوم أنّه يؤدّي على الراحلة، فهو نافلة».

The second premise is a single proposition conjoined with an exception particle (*ḥarf istithnāʾ*), according to the convention of the logicians – such as "but" – or not conjoined, with the discourse pertaining to its meaning.

This second premise includes the mention of one of the two afore-mentioned propositions by way of concession, either in negation or in affirmation, so that it yields either one of the two propositions or their contradictory (*naqīḍ*).

An example of that is: "If the Witr prayer is performed on a riding mount, then it is supererogatory (*nāfilah*). It is known that it is performed on a riding mount. Therefore, it is supererogatory."

وهذا الضرب قسمان:

This kind is twofold.

أحدهما: أن يكون اللازم أعمّ من الملزوم، فينتج على وجهين:

أحدهما: أن يكون الاستثناء عين المقدّم، كقولنا: «إن كانت الصلاة صحيحةً فالمصلّي متطهّر».

وأخـرى: أن يكون الاسـتثناء نقيض التالي كقولنـا: «لكنّه غير متطهّر فالصلاة غير صحيحة».

ولا ينتج استثناء نقيض المقدّم وعين التالي.

The First [Division]: That the consequent be more general than the antecedent. From this, two results may follow.

One: That the exception (*istithnāʾ*) be identical to the antecedent, as in our saying: "If the prayer is valid, then the one performing it is in a state of ritual purity."

Another: That the exception be the contradictory of the consequent, as in our saying: "However, he is not in a state of purification, so the prayer is invalid."

Neither the exception of the contradictory of the antecedent nor the exception of the very consequent yields a conclusion.

القسم الثاني: أن يكونا متساويين، فحينئذٍ ينتج على أربعة أوجه كقولنا: «إن كانت الشمس طالعةً فالنهار موجود»، وذلك لأنّ المتساويين يلزم من إثبات كلّ واحد منهما إثبات الآخر، ومن نفي كلّ واحد منهما نفي الآخر، بخلاف الأعمّ والأخصّ، فإنّه لا يلزم من نفي الأخصّ نفي الأعمّ ولا من إثبات الأخصّ، فلذلك يبطل من إنتاجها وجهان.

The Second Division: That the two be equivalent (*mutasāwiyān*[17]). In that case, the conclusion follows in four modes,[18] as in our saying: "If the sun is up, then the day exists."

This is because, with two equivalent propositions, the affirmation of either necessitates the affirmation of the other, and the negation of either necessitates the negation of the other.

This is unlike the more general and the more specific, for the negation of the more specific does not necessitate the negation of the more general, nor does the affirmation of the more general [necessitate the affirmation of the more specific]. Therefore, two of the modes of conclusion are invalidated in that case.[19]

[3. THE CONDITIONAL DISJOINING SYLLOGISM]

الضرب الثالث: الشرطيّ المنفصل.

ويسمّيه المتكلّمون السبر والتقسيم، ويسمّيه بعض الفقهاء نمط التعانـد، وهـو مركّـب مـن مقدّمتيـن فأكثر يقتـرن بالأولى حـرف منهما

---

17   (Tr:) Here, the equivalence (coextension) of antecedent
       and consequent means all four inferential modes yield valid conclusions.

18   (Tr:) The four modes are: (1) affirming the antecedent, (2) affirming the
       consequent, (3) denying the antecedent, and (4) denying the consequent. All four
       yield valid conclusions when antecedent and consequent are coextensive.
       When the consequent is more general than the antecedent (the first division
       above), only modes (1) and (4) are valid.

19   (Tr:) Refer back to §1.7.

معاندة، بالثانية حرف استثناء أو معناه، ومثاله قولنا: «هذا العدد إمّا زوج وإمّا فرد، ولكنّه زوج فليس بفرد»، وإنتاجه على أربعة أوجه: مثال الأوّل: مـا ذكرنـا، ومثال الثاني: «لكنّه فرد فليس بـزوج»، ومثال الثالث: «لكنّه ليـس بـزوج فهو فـرد»، ومثال الرابع: «لكنّه ليس بفـرد فهو زوج»، وذلك أنّهما قسمان متناقضان، فينتج إثبات كلّ واحد منهما نفي الآخر، ونفي كلّ واحد منهما إثبات الآخر، فتلك أربعة أوجه.

The Third Kind [of Demonstration]: The *conditional disjoining* (*sharṭī munfaṣil*).

The theologians call it *elimination and division* (*sabr wa-taqsīm*), and some jurists call it the *pattern of opposition* (*namṭ al-taʿānud*).

It is composed of two premises or more: The first is joined with a particle indicating opposition, and the second with a particle of exception or its equivalent in meaning.

An example of it is our saying: "This number is either even or odd. But it is even. Therefore, it is not odd."

Its production (*intāj*) occurs in four modes: the first is what we have mentioned; the second: "But it is odd, therefore it is not even"; the third: "But it is not even, therefore it is odd"; the fourth: "But it is not odd, therefore it is even."

This is because they are two contradictory divisions (*aqsām mutanāqiḍān*): The affirmation of each of them entails the negation of the other, and the negation of each of them entails the affirmation of the other. Thus, there are four modes.

ولا يشـترط أن تنحصـر القضيّة في قسـمين، فقد تكـون ثلاثةً وأكثرَ، ويشترط أن يستوي جميعها، كقولنا: «العدد إمّا متساو أو أقلّ أو أكثر»، ومثالـه فـي الفقـه: «إمّـا واجب أو منـدوب أو حرام أو مكـروه أو مباح»، فإثبات واحد من الأقسام يقتضي نفي ما عداه.

It is not required that a proposition be restricted to two divisions; it may be three or more. It is required, however, that all of them be equal in opposition, as in our saying: "A number is either equal, or less, or greater."

An example in jurisprudence is: "It is either obligatory, or recommended, or forbidden, or reprehensible, or permissible." Affirming one of the divisions necessitates the negation of what remains.

SUPPLEMENT تكميل

إذا لم يقم دليل على قضيّة، فقد استدلّ على إثباتها ببطلان نقيضها أو يستدلّ على بطلانها بإثبات نقيضها.

If a proof (*dalīl*) has not been established for a proposition, one may argue for affirming it by refuting its contradictory (*naqīḍ*), or for refuting it by affirming its contradictory.

والقضيتان المتناقضتان هما اللذان إذا صدقت إحداهما كذبت الأخرى وبالعكس، ويشترط أن يكون المحكوم في القضيّتين واحدًا وأن يكون الحكم واحدًا، وحينئذ يصدق الحكم على النقيض.

Contradictory propositions (*qaḍiyyatān mutanāqiḍatān*) are those such that, if one is true, the other is false, and vice versa.

It is required that the one upon whom judgement of made (*maḥkūm*) in both propositions be one, and that the judgement (*ḥukm*) be one. In that case, the judgement applies to the contradictory.

2

ON LINGUISTIC COGNITIONS

الفنّ الثاني من علم الأصول في المعارف اللغويّة

وهي عشرة أبواب:

It comprises ten sections.

<table>
<tr><td>2.1</td><td>ON CONVENTION, USAGE, AND PREDICATION</td><td align="right">الباب الأوّل: في الوضع والاستعمال والحمل</td></tr>
</table>

أمّا الوضع: فهو جعل اللفظ دليلًا على المعنى، وهو قسمين:

١. وضع أوّليّ: وهو الذي لم يسبق بوضع آخر ويُسمّى المرتجل.

٢. ووضع منقول من معنى إلى آخر، وهو على قسمين:

أ. منقول لعلاقة وهو المجاز.

ب. ومنقول لغير علاقة، ويختصّ باسم المنقول كتسمية الولد جعفر والجعفر في اللغة النهر الصغير.

Convention (*waḍʿ*) is the assignment of a term (*lafẓ*) as an indicator (*dalīl*) of a meaning, and it is of two kinds.

1. *Primary convention* (*waḍʿ awwalī*) is that which is not preceded by another convention, and it is called the *improvised* (*murtajal*).
2. *Transferred convention* (*waḍʿ manqūl*) is that which is transferred from one meaning to another, and it is of two kinds:
1. *transferred due to a relation* – this is the figurative (*majāz*), and
2. *transferred without a relation* – this is designated by the name

of the transferred (*manqūl*), such as naming a child Jaʿfar, while *jaʿfar* in language denotes a small river.

وأمّا الاستعمال: فهو التكلّم باللفظ بعد وضعه وسواء أطلق على معناه الأوّل أو نقل عنه لعلاقة أو غير علاقة.

Usage (istiʿmāl) is the utterance of the term after its convention (*waḍ*), whether it is applied to its first meaning, or transferred from it due to a relation, or without a relation.

وأمّا الحمل: فهو اعتقاد السامع لمراد المتكلّم من لفظه سواء أصاب مراده أو أخطأه.

Construal (ḥaml) is the hearer's apprehension of the speaker's intended meaning from his term, whether he is correct in that apprehension or mistaken.

فالاستعمال من صفة المتكلّم، والحمل من صفة السامع، والوضع متقدّم عليها.

Usage pertains to the attribute of the speaker, construal pertains to the attribute of the hearer, and convention precedes them both.

فروع ثلاثة

الأوّل: في واضع اللغات، فذهب قوم إلى أنّها اصطلاحيّة، ووضعهما الناس فيما بينهم ليتخاطبوا بها، وذهب قوم إلى أنّها توقيفيّة وضعها اللّه وعلّمها عباده بواسطة الملائكة والأنبياء.

والأمر في ذلك محتمل ولا تبتغي عليه فائدة.

First Branch: Concerning the originator of languages: One group held that they are conventional (*iṣṭilāḥiyyah*), established by people among themselves in order to communicate. Another group held that they are divinely ordained (*tawqīfiyyah*), instituted by Allah and taught to His servants through the mediation of angels and prophets.

The matter in this is open to possibility, and no benefit is sought in it.

الفرع الثاني: أجاز مالك والشافعيّ استعمال اللفظ الواحد في معنيين فأكثر في حالة واحدة، ومنعه قوم، وذلك كالمشترك، يطلق على معنيين، وكالحقيقـة والمجـاز يجمع بينهما في اللفظ، ومنه قوله تعالى: ﴿إِنَّ اللَّهَ وَمَلَائِكَتَهُ يُصَلُّونَ عَلَى النَّبِيِّ﴾ [الأحزاب ٥٦]، لأنّ الـصلاة من الله الرحمة، ومن الملائكة الدعاء، وقد استعمل في المعنيين معًا.

Second Branch: Mālik and al-Shāfiʿī permitted the use of a single term for two or more meanings in one instance, while others forbade it. This is like the equivocal, which is applied to two meanings, and like combining the literal and figurative in one term.

An example of this is His saying, exalted is He: "Indeed, Allah and His angels send blessings upon the Prophet."[20] For the blessings (*ṣalāh*) from Allah are mercy, and from the angels are supplication. Thus the term has been used for both meanings together.

الفرع الثالث: إذا ورد اللفظ المشترك بقرينة، حمل على المعنى الذي تـدلّ عليـه القرينـة، وإن ورد مجرّدًا عن القرائـن، توقّف فيه، فلم يتصرّف فيه إلّا بدليل.

وقال الشـافعيّ يحمل على جميع محتملاته احتياط والفرق بين هذه الفروع أنّ الأوّل في الوضع والثاني في الاستعمال، والثالث في الحمل.

Third Branch: If an equivocal term appears with a contextual indicator (*qarīnah*), it is construed according to the meaning indicated by the contextual indicator. If it appears devoid of contextual indicators, one suspends judgement concerning it, and it is not acted upon except with proof.

---

20   Qurʾān, 33:56.

Al-Shāfiʿī said: It is construed according to all of its possible meanings as a precaution.

* * *

The distinction between these branches is that the first pertains to convention, the second to usage, and the third to construal.

| 2.2 | ON THE LITERAL AND THE FIGURATIVE | الباب الثاني: في الحقيقة والمجاز |

وفيه فصلان:

It comprises two sections.

| 2.2.1 | ON THEIR DEFINITION | الفصل الأوّل: ففي حدهما |

أمّا الحقيقة: فهي اللفظ المستعمل في معناه.

والمجاز: هو اللفظ المستعمل في غير معناه لعلاقة بينهما.

والمـراد بالمعنـى هنا: هو ما يعنيه العرف الذي وقع التخاطب، وذلك

أنّ الاستعمال على ثلاثة أضرب: لغويّ، وشرعيّ، وعرفيّ.

Literal (ḥaqīqah) is the term employed in its own meaning.

Figurative (majāz) is the term employed in other than its own meaning due to a relation between the two.

What is meant by "meaning" (*maʿnā*) here is what is intended by the custom in which the discourse takes place. For usage is of three kinds: linguistic, legal, and customary.

واللفظ يكون حقيقةً في أحدهما مجازًا في الآخر، وهو تصيير الحقيقة

مجازًا، والمجاز حقيقةً باختلاف الاستعمال، ألا ترى أنّ الدابّة في اللغة

حقيقة في كلّ حيوان، وفي العرف أهل مصر حقيقة في الحمار لا غير،

وفـي عـرف أهل المغرب حقيقة في المركوبـات كلّها، وهي مجاز بالنظر

إلى كلّ استعمال منها إذا أطلقت على سواه.

A term may be literal in one usage and figurative in another. This entails that the literal becomes figurative, and the figurative becomes literal, by difference of usage. Do you not see that *dābbah*, in [the Arabic] language, is literal for every animal, whereas in the convention of the people of Egypt it is literal for the donkey alone, and in the convention of the people of the Maghrib it is literal for all mounts? It is figurative with respect to each of these usages when applied to other than what that usage intends.

وكذلــك الــصلاة والزكاة والصيام وغير ذلك من الألفاظ الشـرعيّة، لها معـانٍ فـي اللغة، ومعانٍ في الشـرع، وهـي بالنظر إلى الشـرع حقيقة في المعاني الشرعيّة مجاز في اللغويّة، وهي بالنظر إلى اللغة بعكس ذلك .

Likewise, prayer (*ṣalāh*), almsgiving (*zakāh*), fasting (*ṣiyām*), and other such legal terms have meanings in [the Arabic language] language and meanings in the law. In relation to the law, they are literal in their legal meanings and figurative in their linguistic ones; and in relation to language, the opposite holds.

<table>
<tr><td>2.2.2   ON THE CATEGORIES OF THE FIGURATIVE</td><td>الفصل الثاني: في أقسام المجاز</td></tr>
</table>

وهو ينقسم قسمين:

١. مجاز في الإفراد، وهو الأكثر .

٢. ومجاز في التركيب والإسناد، كقوله تعالى: ﴿فَمَا رَبِحَتْ تِجَارَتُهُمْ﴾ [البقـرة ١٦] لأنّ الربــح فـي الحقيقـة من صفة التاجـر لا من صفة التجارة .

It is divided into two categories:

1. figurative in individuation (*majāz fī al-ifrād*), and this is the more common; and
2. figurative in composition and predication (*majāz fī al-tarkīb wa-l-isnād*), as in His saying, exalted is He: "So their trade did not

profit,"[21] because profit, literally, is an attribute of the trader, not of the trade.

وينقسم من طريق علاقته عشرة أقسام:

أوّلها: مجاز التشبيه، كتسمية الشجاع بالأسد، وتدخل الاستعارة في هذا القسم.

وثانيها: تسمية المجاور باسم مجاوره.

وثالثها: إطلاق اسم الكلّ على البعض.

ورابعها: إطلاق البعض على الكلّ.

وخامسها: تسمية السبب باسم المسبّب.

It is divided, in terms of its relation, into ten categories:

First: Figurative by resemblance (*majāz al-tashbīh*), such as calling a brave man a lion. Metaphor (*istiʿārah*) falls under this category.

Second: Naming the adjacent by the name of that to which it is adjacent.

Third: Applying the name of the whole to a part.

Fourth: Applying the name of a part to the whole.

Fifth: Naming the cause (*sabab*) by the name of the effect (*musabbab*).

وسادسها: تسمية المسبّب باسم السبب.

وسابعها: التسمية أو الوصف بما يستقبل.

ثامنها: بما مضى.

وتاسعها: الزيادة في اللفظ.

وعاشرها: النقصان منه.

---

21   Qurʾān, 2:16.

Sixth: Naming the effect (*musabbab*) by the name of the cause (*sabab*).

Seventh: Naming or describing by what is to come.

Eighth: Naming or describing by what has passed.

Ninth: Addition in the term.

Tenth: Omission from it.

<table>
<tr><td>2.3</td><td>ON UNIVERSALITY AND PARTICULARITY</td><td>الباب الثالث: في العموم والخصوص</td></tr>
</table>

وفيه ثلاثة فصول:

It comprises three sections.

<table>
<tr><td>2.3.1</td><td>ON THE DEFINITION OF GENERALITY AND ITS INSTRUMENTS</td><td>الفصل الأوّل: في حدّ العموم وأدواته</td></tr>
</table>

أمّـا حدّه فالعموم وهو: شــمول الحكم لكلّ فرد مــن أفراد الحقيقة والعامّ هو: اللفظ الموضوع لمعنى كلّيّ بشرط شمول الحكم لكلّ فرد من أفراده فهو من الكلّيّة لا من الكلّ.

As for its true definition: *Generality* (*ʿumūm*) is the inclusion of the judgement with respect to every individual of the reality.

The *general* (*ʿāmm*) is the term coined for a universal meaning on the condition that the judgement includes every individual of its instances. Thus it pertains to the universal (*kulliyyah*), not to the whole (*kull*).

وأدوات العمــوم: «كلّ»، و «جميــع»، و «أجمــع»، والجمع إذا كان بالألف واللام ســواء كان ســالمًا أو متكسرًا، واسم الجمع كذلك والمفرد إذا كان بالألف واللام التي للجنس، والنكرة في سياق النفي، و «الذي» و «التـي» وتثنيتهمـا وجمعهمـا، و «من»، و «ما»، و «أي»، و «متى» في

الزمان و «أين» و «حيث» في المكان، و «مهما»، وقال الشــافعيّ: ترك الاسـتفصال فــي حكاية الأحوال تقوم مقــام العموم في المقال، واختلف في الفعل في سياق النفي.

The instruments of generality (*adawāt al-ʿumūm*) are:

- *kull* ("all");
- *jamīʿ* ("entirety");
- *ajmaʿ* ("altogether");
- the plural with the definite article *al-* – whether sound or broken;
- the collective noun (*ism al-jamʿ*) likewise;[22]
- the singular with the definite article *al-* of genus;
- the indefinite in the context of negation;
- *alladhī* ("he who"), *allatī* ("she who"), and their dual and plural forms;
- *man* ("whoever");
- *mā* ("whatever");
- *ayy* ("whichever");
- *matā* ("when") in reference to time;
- *ayna* ("where") and *ḥaythu* ("wherever") in reference to place; and
- *mahmā* ("whatever").

Al-Shāfiʿī said: "The omission of specification in the narration of circumstances takes the place of generality in discourse."

There is disagreement regarding the verb in the context of negation.

<table>
<tr><td>

2.3.2 ON THE DEFINITION OF
SPECIFICATION AND THE
MENTION OF SPECIFIERS

</td><td dir="rtl">

الفصل الثاني: في حدّ التخصيص
وذكر المخصّصات

</td></tr>
</table>

أمّا التخصيـص: فهـو إخـراج بعض ما يتناولـه العموم قبل تقـرّر حكمه، وتحرّزنا بهذا القيد من النسخ، لأنّه بحدّ تقرّر الحكم الأوّل.

---

22   (Tr:) i.e. whether sound or broken.

Specification (*takhṣīṣ*) is the exclusion of some of what the generality encompasses before the ruling concerning it is established. By this qualification we guard against abrogation (*naskh*), for abrogation pertains to the point after the initial ruling has been established.

وأمّا المخصّصات للعموم فضربان: متّصلة، ومنفصلة.

The specifiers (*mukhaṣṣiṣāt*) of generality are of two kinds: connected, and disconnected.

فالمتّصلة: الاستثناء، والشرط، والصفة، والغاية.

The connected (*muttasilah*) are: exception (*istithnāʾ*), condition (*sharṭ*), attribute (*ṣifah*), and limit (*ghāyah*).

والمنفصلة: العقـل، والحسّ، ومنطوق الكتاب والسنّة، ومفهومهما، وفعـل النبـيّ -صلّى اللَّه عليه وسـلّم-، وإقراره، والإجمـاع، والقياس على خلاف فيه كلّ هذه تخصّص الكتاب والسنّة.

The disconnected (*munfaṣilah*) are:
- the intellect (*ʿaql*),
- the sense[s] (*ḥiss*),
- the explicit wording of the Book and the Sunnah (*manṭūq*),
- their implied meaning (*mafhūm*),
- the action of the Prophet (may Allah bless him and give him peace),
- his tacit approval,
- consensus (*ijmāʿ*), and
- analogical reasoning (*qiyās*) – though there is disagreement concerning it.

All of these serve to specify the Book and the Sunnah.

ولا يخصّـص العمـوم وروده على سـبب خاصّ خلافًا للشـافعيّ، ولا يخصّصه العرف والعادة على خلاف ذلك، ولا مخالفة راويه له ولا عطفه على خاصّ، ولا عطف خاصّ عليه.

Generality is not specified by its being occasioned by a specific cause – contrary to al-Shāfiʿī; nor by custom or habit; nor by its transmitter acting contrary to it; nor by its being conjoined to a particular; nor by a particular being conjoined to it.

2.3.3   ON MISCELLANEOUS ISSUES   **الفصل الثالث: في مسائل متفرقة**

الأولــى: مذهــب مالــك والقاضــي أبي بكر بــن الطيّـب، أن أقلّ الجمع اثنان، ومذهب الشافعيّ وأبي حنيفة وغيرهما أن أقلّ الجمع ثلاثة.

First: The position of Mālik and al-Qāḍī Abū Bakr ibn al-Ṭayyib is that the minimum of plurality (*jamʿ*) is two, while the position of al-Shāfiʿī, Abū Ḥanīfah, and others is that the minimum of plurality is three.

المسألــة الثانيــة: يتدرج العبيد في خطاب الناس، ويندرج النســاء في خطاب الرجال لاستوائهم في الأحكام إلّا ما خصّصه الدليل.

Second Issue: Slaves are subsumed under the address (*khiṭāb*) directed to people and women are subsumed under the address directed to men, due to their equality in rulings – except where it has been specified by proof.

المسألة الثالثة: يجوز التخصيص حتى لا يبقى من العموم إلّا واحد.

Third Issue: Specification is possible even to the extent that only one instance remains of generality.

المسألة الرابعة: إذا خصّ العامّ، بقي حجّةً بعد التخصيص.

Fourth Issue: If the general is specified, it remains probative (*ḥujjah*) after specification.

المسألة الخامسة: إذا ورد الاستثناء أو الشرط أو الغاية بعد أشياء فمذهب مالك: أنّه يرجع إلى جميعها، ومذهب أبي حنيفة أنّه يرجع إلى الأخير خاصّةً.

Fifth Issue: If an exception, or a condition, or a limit follows multiple items, the school of Mālik holds that it applies to all of them, while the school of Abū Ḥanīfah holds that it applies only to the last.

تقسيم الألفاظ أربعة أقسام:

١. عامّ أُريد به العموم نحو: «كلّ مسكر حرام»،

٢. وخاصّ أُريد به الخصوص كقوله -صلّى اللّه عليه وسلّم- في الذهب والحرير: «هَذَانِ مُحَرَّمَانِ عَلَى ذُكُورِ أُمَّتِي»،

٣. وعامّ أُريد به الخصوص كقوله تعالى: ﴿الزَّانِيَةُ وَالزَّانِي فَاجْلِدُوا﴾ [النور ٢]، فإنّه يراد به غير المحصن،

٤. وخاصّ أُريد به العموم كقوله تعالى: ﴿فَلَا تَقُلْ لَهُمَا أُفٍّ﴾ [الإسراء ٢٣] فإنّ المراد النهي عن أنواع العقوق كلّها.

Terms are categorised into four categories

1. A general intended as general (*ʿāmm urīda bihi al-ʿumūm*), such as "Every intoxicant is forbidden."[23]

2. A particular intended as particular (*khāṣṣ urīda bihi al-khuṣūṣ*), such as his – may Allah bless him and give him peace – statement regarding gold and silk: "These two are forbidden for the males of my community."[24]

3. A general intended as particular (*ʿāmm urīda bihi al-khuṣūṣ*), such

---

23   From Anas: Aḥmad, 12217; al-Ḍiyāʾ, 1538 – he said: its *isnād* is sound.
From Abū Mūsā: Aḥmad, 19743; al-Bukhārī, 6751; Muslim, 1733; Abū Dāwūd, 3684; al-Nasāʾī, 5595; Ibn Mājah, 3391.

24   From: ʿAlī ibn Abī Ṭālib: Aḥmad, 750; Abū Dāwūd, 4057; al-Nasāʾī, 5144; Ibn Mājah, 3595; al-Bayhaqī, 4019; Ibn Abī Shaybah, 24659; al-Bazzār 886; Abū Yaʿlā, 272; Ibn Ḥibbān 5434.

as His saying, exalted is He: "The woman and the man guilty of fornication, flog each one of them,"[25] for what is intended is the non-married fornicator.

4. A particular intended as general (*khāṣṣ urīda bihi al-ʿumūm*), such as His saying, exalted is He: "Do not say to them '*uff*,'"[26] for what is intended is the prohibition of all forms of filial impiety.

2.4   ON EXCEPTION

الباب الرابع: في الاستثناء

وفيه فصلان:

It comprises two sections.

2.4.1 ON ITS DEFINITION

الفصل الأوّل: في حدّه

قال بعضهم: هو إخراج الأوّل عما دخل فيه الثاني بـ «إلّا» ونحوها.

وقيـل: هـو إخـراج بعض مـا يتوهّـم دخوله فـي اللفـظ الأوّل بأدوات الاستثناء مع ما بعدها حتى يصل بما قبلها.

Some have said: *Exception* (*istithnāʾ*) is the exclusion from the first of that which the second has entered, by "except" and the like.

And it was said: It is the exclusion of some of what is imagined to be included in the first term, by means of the instruments of exception together with what follows them, so that it connects with what precedes them.

وتحـرّز بوصـف أدواته من التخصيص، وخرج عند الاستثناء المنقطع لأنّه لا يتوهّم دخوله في اللفظ الأوّل، كقولك: «جاءني القوم إلّا حماراً»، فإنّ الحمـار لا يتوهّـم دخولـه فـي القـوم، وذلك أنّ الاستثناء على أربعة أنواع:

---

25   Qurʾān, 24:2.

26   Qurʾān, 17:23.

He guarded, by describing its instruments,[27] against confusing it with specification (*takhṣīṣ*). It is excluded in the case of the disconnected exception (*istithnāʾ munqaṭiʿ*), because its inclusion in the first term is not presumed – such as your saying: "The people came to me, except a donkey," for the donkey is not presumed to be included among the people.

That is because exception is of four kinds:

(١) تـارةً يُخـرج مـا لـولاه لعلم دخوله، وهو الاسـتثناء مـن النصوص كقولك: «عندي عشرة إلّا اثنين».

(1) At times, that which – were it not excluded – its inclusion would be known; and this is the exception from explicit texts (*nuṣūṣ*),[28] such as our statement: "I have ten – except for two."

(٢) تـارةً يخـرج مـا لـولاه لظنّ دخولـه، وهو الاسـتثناء مـن الظواهر والعمومات نحو: «اقتلوا الكفار إلّا النساء والصبيان».

(2) At times, that which – were it not excluded – its inclusion would be presumption (*ẓann*), is excluded; and this is the exception from apparent terms (*ẓawāhir*) and generalities (*ʿumūmāt*), such as "Kill the disbelievers – except women and children."

(٣) وتـارةً يخـرج مـا لولاه لجاز دخوله، وهو الاسـتثناء مـن الأزمان، نحـو: «صلّ إلّا عند طلوع الشـمس»، ومن المـكان، نحو: «اجلس إلّا علـى المقابـر»، ومن الأحوال، نحـو: ﴿لَتَأْتُنَّنِي بِهِ إِلَّا أَنْ يُحَاطَ بِكُمْ﴾ [يوسف ٦٦].

(3) At times, that which – were it not excluded – its inclusion would have been possible. This is the exception pertaining to times, such as "Pray – except at sunrise"; places, such as "Sit – except on

---

27   (Tr:) i.e. "except" (*illā*) and its likes.
28   See §2.6.1.

graves"; and states, such as "You will surely bring him to me – except if you are surrounded."[29]

(٤) وتارةً يخرج ما يقطع بعدم دخوله، وهو الاستثناء المنقطع، لأنّ الثاني من غير جنس الأوّل. واختلف فيه هل حقيقة أو مجاز، فإن جعلناه مجازًا، فالحدّ صحيح لأنّ الحدود إنّما توضع للحقائق، وإن جعلناه حقيقةً، فيزاد في الحدّ أو ما يعرض في نفس المتكلّم والسامع ليشمل المنقطع.

(4) At times, that which is decisively known not to be included is excluded; this is the disconnected exception, because the second is not of the genus of the first. There is a disagreement concerning it – whether it is literal or figurative.

If we consider it figurative, then the true definition is sound, because definitions are only established for literals. But if we consider it literal, then an addition must be made to the definition, or to what occurs in the mind of the speaker and the hearer, so that the disconnected may be encompassed.

2.4.2 ON MISCELLANEOUS ISSUES   **الفصل الثاني: في مسائل متفرقة**

الأولى: الاستثناء من الإثبات نفي، ومن النفي إثبات.

First: Exception from affirmation is negation, and exception from negation is affirmation.

الثانية: يجوز استثناء الأكثر من الجملة خلافًا للقاضي أبي بكر بن الطيّب.

Second: It is possible to except the greater part from the whole sentence, contrary to the view of Qāḍī Abū Bakr ibn al-Ṭayyib.

---

29   Qurʾān, 12:66.

الثالثة : يجوز أن يكون الاستثناء متّصلًا بالمستثنى منه، وحكي عن ابن عبّاس جـوازه ولو بعد شـهر. والتحقيق أنّ قول ابن عبّاس ليس في الاستثناء «بإلّا» ونحوها وإنّما هو في الاستثناء في اليمين بمشيئة اللَّه.

Third: It is possible for the exception to be connected to the excepted-from (*mustathnā minhu*).

It has been reported from Ibn ʿAbbās that he permitted it even after a month. The correct view is that the statement of Ibn ʿAbbās does not pertain to exception with "except" (*illā*) and the like, but rather to exception in oaths by the will of Allah (*bi-mashīʾat Allāh*).

<table>
<tr><td>

2.5   ON THE ABSOLUTE AND
THE QUALIFIED

</td><td>

الباب الخامس: في المطلق والمقيّد

</td></tr>
</table>

وفيه فصلان :

It comprises two sections.

<table>
<tr><td>

2.5.1 ON THEIR MEANING

</td><td>

الفصل الأوّل: في معناهما

</td></tr>
</table>

فالمطلـق : هـو الكلّـيّ الذي لم يدخلـه تقيد، فلذلك لا يكـون إلّا نكرةً لشياعها، وليكتفي في الحكم عليه بفرد من أفراده، أي فرد كان.

والمقيّد : هو الذي دخله تعيين ولو من بعض الوجوه، كالشرط والصفة وغير ذلك.

The *absolute* (*muṭlaq*) is the universal that has not undergone qualification (*taqyīd*). Therefore, it is only indefinite, due to its diffuseness; it suffices in judgement to apply it to one of its individuals, whichever it may be.

The *qualified* (*muqayyad*) is that which has undergone specification (*taʿyīn*), even if only from some aspects – such as a condition (*sharṭ*), an attribute (*ṣifah*), and the like.

والتقييـد والإطلاق أمـران إضافيّـان، فربّ مطلقٍ مقيَّدٌ بالنسـبة، وربّ مقيَّدٌ مطلقٍ. فإذا قلتَ «إنسان» فهو مطلق، ولو قلتَ فيه «حيوان ناطق» لـكان مقيَّدًا لوصـف الحيوان بالنطـق، وقد يكون اللفـظ مقيَّدًا من وجه مطلقًا من وجه كقولك: «أُكرم رجلًا صالحًا»، فإنّه مقيَّد بالصلاح مطلق في غير ذلك من الصفات كالبياض والسواد.

Restriction (*taqyīd*) and absoluteness (*iṭlāq*) are two relative matters, for what is absolute may be qualified in relation, and what is restricted may be absolute.

So if you say "human," it is absolute. But if you say "a rational animal," it becomes restricted by describing "animal" with "rational."

A term may be qualified in one respect and absolute in another, such as your saying: "Honour a righteous man." It is restricted by righteousness, yet absolute with respect to other attributes, such as whiteness or blackness.

2.5.2 ON THEIR RULINGS — الفصل الثاني: في أحكامهما

إذا ورد الخطاب مطلقًا لا مقيّدًا له حمل على إطلاقه، وإن ورد مقيّدًا لا مطلـق لـه حمل على تقييـده، وإن ورد مطلقًا في موضع ومقيّدًا في آخر، فإن ذلك ينقسم إلى أربعة أقسام:

If discourse is presented in an absolute form without any qualification, it is construed according to its absoluteness.

If it is presented in a qualified form without any absolute counterpart, it is construed according to its qualification.

If it is presented in an absolute form in one instance and in a qualified form in another, then this is divided into four categories:

الأوّل: متّفـق الحكـم والسـبب، كتقييـد الغنم بالسَّـيوم في حديث، وإطلاقها في آخر فهذا يحمل فيه المطلق على المقيّد.

First: When the ruling (*ḥukm*) and the cause (*sabab*) are identical, such as the qualifying of sheep to pasturing in one ḥadīth[30] and their absolute mention in another[31] – in this, the absolute is construed according to the qualified.

ومتّحد الحكم مختلف السـبب، كالرقبة المعتقة في الكفّارة، قُيِّدت فـي القتـل بالإيمان وأطلقت في الظهار، فاختلف هل يحمل فيه المطلق على المقيّد أم لا؟

[Second:] United in ruling yet differing in cause, such as the emancipated slave in an expiation: it is qualified by faith (*īmān*) in the case of homicide, and absolute in the case of *ẓihār*.[32] There is a divergence here – whether the absolute is construed according to the qualified in this case, or not.

ومختلـف الحكم متّحد السـبب، كتقييـد الوضوء بالمرافـق وإطلاق التيمّم، والسبب فيهما واحد، وهو الحدث، فاختلف فيه أيضًا، ومذهب الشـافعيّ حمـل المطلق علـى المقيّد فـي هذين القسـمين خلافًا لأبي حنيفة، واختلف فيه أصحاب مالك.

[Third:] Differing in ruling yet united in cause, such as the qualification of ablution (*wuḍū*) to the elbows and the absoluteness of dry ablution (*tayammum*),[33] though their cause is one – namely, ritual impurity (*ḥadath*). There is disagreement in this as well.

The school of al-Shāfiʿī holds that the absolute is construed according to the qualified in these two cases, contrary to Abū Ḥanīfah, while the companions of Mālik differed in it.

---

30   Abū Dāwūd, 1567.

31   Abū Dāwūd, 1568.

32   (Tr:) Declaring that one's wife resembles one's mother.

33   Qur'an, 5:6.

والرابع: مختلف الحكم مختلف السبب، فلا يحمل فيه المطلق على المقيّد إجماعًا.

Fourth: Differing in ruling and differing in cause – the absolute is not construed according to the qualified, by consensus (*ijmā'*).

<table>
<tr><td>

2.6   ON THE TEXT, THE APPARENT, THE INTERPRETED, AND THE CLARIFIED

</td><td>

الباب السادس: في النصّ والظاهر والمؤوّل والمبيّن

</td></tr>
</table>

وفيه فصلان:

It comprises two sections.

<table>
<tr><td>

2.6.1   ON THE MEANING OF THESE TERMS

</td><td>

الفصل الأوّل: في معنى هذه الألفاظ

</td></tr>
</table>

ولذكرها بتقسيم وهو أنّ اللفظ إن دلّ على معنى ولم يحتمل غيره، فهو النصّ، على أنّ أكثر فقهاء الزمان يقولون النصّ في المحتمل وغيره.

وإن احتمل معنيين فأكثر، فلا يخلو إمّا أن يكون أحدهما أرجحَ من الآخر أم لا، فإن كان أحدهما أرجحَ من الآخر سُمّي بالنظر إلى الراجح ظاهرًا، وبالنسبة إلى المرجوح أو الأخفى مؤوّلًا، وهو مشتقّ من التأويل، ومعناه: إخراج اللفظ عن ظاهره، وإن لم يترجّح أحـد الاحتمالين على الآخر فهو المجمل.

To mention it by division, namely: If a term indicates a meaning and does not admit another, it is the *explicit text* (*naṣṣ*) – although most jurists of the time say that *naṣṣ* applies also to that which admits another meaning.

If it bears two or more meanings, then either one of them is more preponderant than the other or not.

If one is more preponderant, then with respect to the preponderant meaning it is called the *apparent* (*ẓāhir*), and with respect to the less preponderant or more obscure meaning it is called the *interpreted* (*muʾawwal*). This is derived from interpretation (*taʾwīl*), meaning the removal of the term from its apparent meaning.

If neither of the two possibilities is preponderant over the other, then it is the *ambiguous* (*mujmal*).

وأمّا المبيَّن: فهو ما أفاد معناه إمّا بالوضع أو بضميمة تبيينه وهو يشمل النصّ والظاهر، فهو نقيض المجمل.

Clarified (*mubayyan*) is that which conveys its meaning either by convention (*waḍʿ*) or by an adjunct that clarifies it, and it includes the explicit text and the apparent. Thus, it is the contradictory of the ambiguous.

2.6.2 ON MISCELLANEOUS ISSUES الفصل الثاني: في مسائل متفرقة

المسألة الأولى: البيان يقع بالقول وبالمفهوم وبالكتابة، وبالإشارة وبالقياس وبالدليل العقليّ والحسّيّ وبالتعليل.

First Issue: Clarification (*bayān*) occurs through speech, the sense (*mafhūm*), writing, indication (*ishārah*), analogy (*qiyās*), rational and sensory proof (*dalīl ʿaqlī wa-ḥissī*), and through reasoning (*taʿlīl*).

المسألة الثانية: وقع المجمل في الكتاب والسنّة خلافًا لقوم.

Second Issue: The ambiguous does occur in the Book and the Sunnah, contrary to the view of some.

المسألة الثالثة: إضافة التحليل والتحريم إلى الأعيان ليس مجملًا، فيحمل على ما يدلّ عليه الحرف في كلّ عين، فقوله تعالى: ﴿حُرِّمَتْ

عَلَيْكُمْ أُمَّهَاتُكُمْ﴾ [النساء ٢٣] محمول على النكاح، وقوله: ﴿حُرِّمَتْ
عَلَيْكُمُ الْمَيْتَةُ﴾ [المائدة ٣] محمول على الأكل.

Third Issue: The attribution of permissibility and prohibition to entities is not ambiguous. Rather, it is to be construed according to what the particle (*ḥarf*) indicates in each case.

Thus, His saying, exalted is He: "Prohibited to you are your mothers"[34] is to be understood as pertaining to marriage, and His saying: "Prohibited to you is carrion"[35] is to be understood as pertaining to eating.

المسألة الرابعة: لا يجوز تأخير البيان عن وقت الحاجة، ويجوز تأخيره
عن وقت الخطاب.

Fourth Issue: Clarification may not be delayed beyond the time of need, but it may be delayed beyond the time of address.

<table>
<tr><td>2.7</td><td>ON THE ELLIPTICAL
IMPLICATION OF THE
DISCOURSE, ITS IMPORT,
AND ITS SIGNIFICATION</td><td>الباب السابع: في لحن الخطاب
وفحواه ودليله</td></tr>
</table>

أمَّا لحـن الخطـاب: فهو ما حذف من الكلام ولا يستقلّ المعنى إلّا به
كقوله تعالى: ﴿فَأَوْحَيْنَا إِلَى مُوسَى أَنِ اضْرِبْ بِعَصَاكَ الْبَحْرَ فَانْفَلَقَ﴾
[الشعراء ٦٣] تقديره: فضرب فانفلق، ومثله: ﴿فَمَنْ كَانَ مِنْكُمْ مَرِيضًا
أَوْ عَلَى سَفَرٍ فَعِدَّةٌ مِنْ أَيَّامٍ أُخَرَ﴾ [البقرة ١٨٤] تقديره: إن أفطر في
المرض أو السفر، وأخذ به العلماء كلّهم إلّا الظاهريّة.

---

34   Qur'ān, 4:23.
35   Qur'ān, 5:3.

Elliptical implication of the discourse (laḥn al-khiṭāb) is that which is omitted from speech, while the meaning does not stand independently without it.

Such as His saying, exalted is He: "So We revealed to Moses: 'Strike the sea with your staff,' and it parted"[36] – its estimation is: "So he struck it, and it parted."

Likewise, His saying: "So whoever among you is ill or on a journey, then a number of other days"[37] – its estimation is: "If he breaks the fast due to illness or travel."

The scholars all accepted this, except the Ẓāhiriyyah.

وأمّا فحوى الخطاب، فيُسمّى تنبيه الخطاب، ومفهوم الموافقة، وهو إثبات حكم المنطوق به للمسكوت عنه بطريق الأولى، وأخذ به العلماء أيضًا إلّا الظاهريّة.

Import of the discourse (faḥwā al-khiṭāb) is also called the *indication of the discourse (tanbīh al-khiṭāb)* and the *concordant inferred meaning (mafhūm al-muwāfaqah)* – namely: the establishment of the ruling of the spoken (*manṭūq*) for the unspoken (*maskūt ʿanhu*) by way of greater reason. The scholars also acted upon it, except the Ẓāhiriyyah.

وهو نوعان:

(١) تنبيه بالأقلّ على الأكثر كقوله تعالى: ﴿فَلَا تَقُلْ لَهُمَا أُفٍّ﴾ [الإسراء ٢٣] فإنّه نبّه بالنهي عن قول «أف» على النهي عن الشتم والضرب وغير ذلك. ومثله قوله تعالى: ﴿مَنْ إِنْ تَأْمَنْهُ بِدِينَارٍ لَا يُؤَدِّهِ إِلَيْكَ﴾ [آل عمران ٦٥].

---

36   Qurʾān, 26:63.

37   Qurʾān, 2:184.

(٢) وتنبيه بالأكثر على الأقلّ كقوله تعالى: ﴿مَنْ إِنْ تَأْمَنْهُ بِقِنْطَارٍ يُؤَدِّهِ إِلَيْكَ﴾ [آل عمران ٧٥].

It is of two kinds.

(1) Indication by the lesser to the greater (*tanbīh bi-l-aqall ʿalā al-akthar*), as in His saying, exalted is He: "So do not say to them ʿ*uff*."[38] For He indicated by prohibiting the utterance of "uff" the prohibition of reviling, striking, and the like. And likewise His saying, exalted is He: "One whom, if you entrust with a single dinar, he will not return it to you."[39]

(2) Indication by the greater to the lesser (*tanbīh bi-l-akthar ʿalā al-aqall*), as in His saying, exalted is He: "Whomever you entrust with a *qinṭār*, he will return it to you."[40]

أمّا دليل الخطاب: فهو مفهوم المخالفة، وهو الذي يطلق الفقهاء عليه اسم المفهوم في الأكثر، وهو إثبات نقيض حكم المنطوق به للمسكوت عنه، وهو حجّة عند مالك والشافعيّ خلافًا لأبي حنيفة.

وكلّ مفهوم فله منطوق، ولا خلاف أنّ المنطوق حجّة لأنّه الذي وضع له اللفظ، مثال ذلك: «إِنَّما الوَلَاءَ لِمَنْ أَعْتَقَ»، فمنطوق هذا اللفظ إثبات الولاء لمن أعتق، ومفهومه نفي الولاء عمن لم يعتق.

Signification of the discourse (*dalīl al-khiṭāb*) is the *contrary sense* (*mafhūm al-mukhālafah*), which the jurists most often call simply "the sense" (*mafhūm*). It is the establishment of the opposite ruling of the spoken for the unspoken. It is probative (*ḥujjah*) according to Mālik and al-Shāfiʿī, contrary to Abū Ḥanīfah.

Every sense (*mafhūm*) has a spoken, and there is no disagreement that the spoken is probative, for it is that for which the term was

---

38   Qurʾān, 17:23.
39   Qurʾān, 3:75.
40   Qurʾān, 3:75.

instituted. An example of this is His saying: "Loyalty (*walāʾ*) is only for the one who manumits."[41]

The spoken of this term is the affirmation of loyalty to the one who manumits, and its sense is the negation of loyalty from the one who does not manumit.

وهو عشرة أنواع:

It [the contrary sense] is of ten kinds.

(١) مفهـوم العلّة: نحو: «مَا أُسْـكَرَ فَهُوَ حَـرَامٌ»، فمنطوق هذا اللفظ تحريم المسكر، ومفهومه تحليل غير المسكر.

(٢) ومفهوم الصفة: نحو «فِي سَائِمَةِ الْغَنَمِ الزَّكَاةُ».

الفرق بين العلّة والصفة، أنّ العلّة سبب الحكم بخلاف الصفة.

(1) The contrary sense of the cause (*mafhūm al-ʿillah*), such as "Whatever intoxicates is forbidden."[42] The spoken (*manṭūq*) of this term is the prohibition of the intoxicant, and its sense (*mafhūm*) is the permissibility of that which does not intoxicate.

(2) The contrary sense of the attribute (*mafhūm al-ṣifah*), such as "In pasturing livestock there is alms."[43]

---

41   From Ibn ʿUmar: Mālik, 1478; Aḥmad, 5761; al-Bukhārī, 2048; Abū Dāwūd, 3930.

      From Ibn ʿAbbās: al-Ṭabarānī, 11744.

42   Abū Yaʿlā, 3971.

43   Ibn Ḥajar in _Al-Talkhīṣ al-Ḥabīr:

      The ḥadīth: "In freely-grazing sheep, zakāh is due." Al-Bukhārī has it in the ḥadīth of Anas with the wording: "Regarding the zakāh on sheep – in those freely-grazing, from forty to one hundred and twenty: one ewe." The compiler mentioned it shortly after, from the ḥadīth of Anas. In the transmission of Abū Dāwūd: "In freely-grazing sheep, if they number..." – and he mentioned it. What al-Rāfiʿī's wording implies – that the ḥadīth of Anas is distinct from this one – is rejected. Ibn al-Ṣalāḥ said: "I believe the jurists' and uṣūlīs' statement 'In freely-grazing sheep, zakāh is due' is an abridgement on their part." End. Abū Dāwūd and al-Nasāʾī also have it from the ḥadīth of Bahz ibn Ḥakīm,

The difference between the cause (*'illah*) and the attribute (*ṣifah*) is that the cause is the reason for the ruling, whereas the attribute is not necessarily so.

(٣) ومفهوم الشرط: نحو: «من تطهّر صحّت صلاته».

(٤) ومفهوم الاستثناء: نحو: «قام القوم إلّا زيدًا».

(٥) ومفهوم الغاية: نحو: ﴿أَتِمُّوا الصِّيَامَ إِلَى اللَّيْلِ﴾ [البقرة ١٨٧].

(3) The contrary sense of the condition (*mafhūm al-sharṭ*), such as "Whoever performs ablution, his prayer is valid."

(4) The contrary sense of exception (*mafhūm al-istithnā'*), such as "The people stood up except Zayd."

(5) The sense of the limit (*ghāyah*), such as His saying, exalted is He: "Complete the fast until the night."[44]

(٦) ومفهوم الحصر: نحو: «إنّما الولاء لمن أعتق».

وأدوات الحصـر أربعـة: «إنّما»، وتقـدّم النفي قبل أدوات الاسـتثناء، وتقدّم المعمولات، والمبتدأ مع الخبر.

(6) The contrary sense of restriction (*mafhūm al-ḥaṣr*), such as "Loyalty (*walā'*) is only for the one who manumits."[45]

The instruments of restriction (*adawāt al-ḥaṣr*) are four: *innamā*; the precedence of negation before the instruments of exception; the precedence of the objects (*ma'mūlāt*) before the governing term; and the restriction effected by a subject with its predicate.

(٧) ومفهوم الزمان: نحو ﴿قُمِ اللَّيْلَ إِلَّا قَلِيلًا﴾ [المزمل ٢].

---

from his father, from his grandfather, as a raised report (marfū'): "In every freely-grazing camel..." – the ḥadīth.

 Ibn Ḥajar al-ʿAsqalānī, Aḥmad ibn ʿAlī (d. 852/1449). Al-Talkhīṣ al-ḥabīr fī takhrīj aḥādīth al-Rāfiʿī al-kabīr. Edited by Abū ʿĀṣim Ḥasan ibn ʿAbbās ibn Quṭb. Cairo: Muʾassasat Qurṭubah, 1416/1995. 2:306–7.

44 Qurʾān, 2:187.

45 Its sourcing preceded.

(٨) ومفهوم المكان: نحو: ﴿وَأَنْتُمْ عَاكِفُونَ فِي الْمَسَاجِدِ﴾ [البقرة ١٨٧].

(٩) ومفهوم العدد: نحو: ﴿فَاجْلِدُوهُمْ ثَمَانِينَ جَلْدَةً﴾ [النور ٤].

(١٠) ومفهـوم اللقـب: وهو تعليق الحكم على مجرّد أسـماء الذوات نحو: «فِي الغَنَم الزَّكاةُ».

(7) The contrary sense of time (*mafhūm al-zamān*), such as His saying, exalted is He: "Stand [for prayer] the night, except a little."[46]

(8) The contrary sense of place (*mafhūm al-makān*), such as His saying, exalted is He: "while you are secluded in the mosques."[47]

(9) The contrary sense of number (*mafhūm al-ʿadad*), such as His saying, exalted is He: "So flog them with eighty lashes."[48]

(10) The contrary sense of epithet (*mafhūm al-laqab*) is the attaching of a ruling to the mere names of essences, such as "In sheep there is alms."

وأقواهـا مفهـوم العلّـة، وأضعفها مفهـوم اللقـب، ولم يقل بـه أحد إلّا الدَّقاق وخالف في مفهوم الصفة القاضي أبو بكر بن الطيّب وأبو المعالي.

The strongest of them is the [contrary] sense of the cause (*ʿillah*), and the weakest is the sense of the epithet (*laqab*). None held by it except al-Daqqāq, and al-Qāḍī Abū Bakr ibn al-Ṭayyib and Abū al-Maʿālī dissented regarding the sense of the attribute (*ṣifah*).

BRANCH   فرع

إذا خــرج المفهــوم مخرج الغالب فليـس بحجّة إجماعًا نحو: ﴿وَلَا تَقْتُلُوا أَوْلَادَكُمْ خَشْيَةَ إِمْلَاقٍ﴾ [الإسراء ٣١].

---

46   Qurʾān, 73:2.
47   Qurʾān, 2:187.
48   Qurʾān, 24:4.

If the sense (*mafhūm*) is expressed in the manner of what is predominant, then it is not probative (*ḥujjah*) by consensus – such as His saying, exalted is He: "And do not kill your children for fear of poverty."[49]

2.8 ON THE CONFLICT OF THE REQUIREMENTS OF TERMS	الباب الثامن: في تعارض مقتضيات الألفاظ

وفيه فصلان:

It comprises two sections.

2.8.1 ON THE CONFLICT BETWEEN A PREPONDERANT POSSIBILITY AND AN OUTWEIGHED POSSIBILITY	الفصل الأوّل: في تعارض احتمال راجح مع احتمال مرجوح

فيقدّم الراجح، ويحمل الكلام عليه إلّا إن دلّ دليل على إرادة المرجوح، فحينئذٍ يحمل عليه، وإلّا تقدّم الراجح لأنّه الأصل، فتقدم الحقيقة على المجـاز، والعمـوم على الخصوص، والإفراد على الاشـتراك، والاسـتقلال علـى الإضمار، والإطلاق على التقييـد، والتأصيل على الزيادة، والترتيب علـى التقديـم والتأخيـر، والتأسـيس علـى التأكيد، والبقاء على النسـخ، والشرعيّ على العقليّ، والعرفيّ على اللغويّ.

The preponderant (*rājiḥ*) is given precedence, and the discourse is construed accordingly – unless there is proof of intending the outweighed (*marjūḥ*). In that case, it is construed accordingly. Otherwise, the preponderant is given precedence, for it is the default.

Thus precedence is given to: the literal over the figurative, generality over specificity, the univocal over the equivocal, independence over ellipsis, absoluteness over qualification, the authentic over the superfluous, sequence over inversion, establishment over emphasis,

---

49   Qur'ān, 17:31.

continuity over abrogation, the legal over the rational and, the customary over the linguistic.

<table>
<tr><td>

2.8.2   ON THE CONFLICT OF TWO OUTWEIGHED POSSIBILITIES

</td><td>

الفصل الثاني: في تعارض احتمالين مرجوحين

</td></tr>
</table>

فيُقدّم التخصيـص والمجـاز والإضمـار والنقل والاشـتراك على النسـخ، وتقـدّم الأربعة الأوّل على الاشـتراك، والثلاثـة الأوّل على النقل، والأولان علـى الإضمـار، ويقدّم التخصيـص على المجاز خلافًا لفخر الدين بن الخطيب.

Precedence is given to specification, the figurative, ellipsis, transference, and equivocality over abrogation. The first four are given precedence over equivocality; the first three over transference; the first two over ellipsis. Specification is given precedence over the figurative, contrary to Fakhr al-Dīn ibn al-Khaṭīb.

<table>
<tr><td>

BRANCH

</td><td>

فرع

</td></tr>
</table>

إذا تعارضـت الحقيقـة المرجوحة والمجاز الراجـح، قدّمت الحقيقة عند أبي حنيفة، والمجاز عند أبي يوسف، وتوقّف في ذلك فخر الدين.

If the outweighed literal and the preponderant figurative are in conflict, the literal is given precedence according to Abū Ḥanīfah, the figurative according to Abū Yūsuf, and Fakhr al-Dīn suspended judgement in this.

<table>
<tr><td>

2.9   ON THE COMMAND AND THE PROHIBITION

</td><td>

الباب التاسع: في الأمر والنهي

</td></tr>
</table>

وفيه فصلان:

It comprises two sections.

   الفصل الأوّل: في الأمر

إذا ورد مجـرّدًا عــن القرائن حمل على الوجوب عند مالك وأكثر العلماء، وقيل على الندب.

وإن ورد بقرينـة حمـل على مـا تدلّ عليه القرينة مـن الوجوب كقوله: ﴿وَأَقِيمُـوا الـصَّلَاةَ وَآتُـوا الـزَّكَاةَ﴾ [البقـرة ٤٣]، أو النـدب كقولـه: ﴿فَكَاتِبُوهُـمْ﴾ [النور ٣٣]. أو الإباحة كقوله: ﴿وَإِذَا حَلَلْتُمْ فَاصْطَادُوا﴾ [المائـدة ٢] لأنّـه إذا ورد بعد الحظر فهو للإباحة على الأصحّ، وقد يرد للتعجيـز نحـو: ﴿فَأْتُوا بِسُـورَةٍ مِـنْ مِثْلِهِ﴾ [البقـرة ٢٣]، وللتهديد نحو: ﴿اعْمَلُـوا مَا شِـئْتُمْ﴾ [فصلت ٤٠]، وللخبر نحـو: ﴿فَلْيَمْدُدْ لَهُ الرَّحْمَنُ مَدًّا﴾ [مريم ٧٥] كما أنّ الخبر قد يأتي بمعنى الأمر نحو: ﴿وَالْوَالِدَاتُ يُرْضِعْنَ أَوْلَادَهُنَّ﴾ [البقرة ٢٣٣].

If the command (*amr*) appears without contextual indicators (*qarāʾin*), it is construed according to obligation (*wujūb*) according to Mālik and most scholars; it is also said that it is construed according to recommendation (*nadb*).

If it is accompanied by a contextual indicator, it is construed according to what the indicator signifies:

- obligation (*wujūb*), as in His saying, exalted is He: "And establish the prayer and give the alms";[50]
- recommendation (*nadb*), as in His saying, exalted is He: "Then write a contract with them";[51]
- permissibility (*ibāḥah*), as in His saying, exalted is He: "And when you are released [from *iḥrām*], then hunt,"[52] because when it occurs after prohibition it denotes permissibility, according to the sounder opinion;

---

50   Qurʾān, 2:43.
51   Qurʾān, 24:33.
52   Qurʾān, 5:2.

- incapacitation (*taʿjīz*), as in His saying, exalted is He: "Then produce a sūrah like it";[53]
- threat (*tahdīd*), as in His saying, exalted is He: "Do whatever you will";[54]
- declarative (*khabar*), as in His saying, exalted is He: "Then the All-Merciful will extend for him an extension."[55]

Just as a declarative (*khabar*) may come in the sense of a command (*amr*), such as His saying, exalted is He: "Mothers shall suckle their children."[56]

BRANCHES

فروع

الأوّل: الأمر يدلّ على إجزاء المأمور به عند الجمهور.

First: The command indicates the sufficiency (*ijzāʾ*) of the commanded act according to the majority.

الثاني: اختلف هل يقتضي الأمر فعل المأمور به على الفور أم لا؟.

Second: There is a disagreement as to whether the command necessitates immediacy (*fawr*) or not.

الثالث: اختلف هل يقتضي التكرار أم لا؟

Third: There is a disagreement as to whether it necessitates repetition (*takrār*) or not.

الرابع: إذا نسخ الأمر، فاختلف هل يحتجّ به على الجواز أم لا؟.

Fourth: If the command is abrogated, there is a disagreement as to whether it may be used as proof (*yuḥtajj bihi*) for permissibility or not.

---

53 Qurʾān, 2:23.
54 Qurʾān, 41:40.
55 Qurʾān, 19:75.
56 Qurʾān, 2:233.

2.9.2   ON PROHIBITION

الفصل الثاني: في النهي

إذا ورد مجـرّدًا عـن القرائن حمل علـى التحريم عند مالك وأكثر العلماء، وقيـل علـى الكراهـة، وإذا ورد بقرينـة حمل على ما تـدلّ عليه القرينة من تحريم أو كراهة.

If it appears without contextual indicators, it is construed according to prohibition (*taḥrīm*) according to Mālik and most scholars; it is also said that it is construed according to reprehensibility (*karāhah*).

If it appears with a contextual indicator, it is construed according to what the indicator denotes – whether prohibition or reprehensibility.

BRANCHES

فروع

الأوّل: النهـي يـدلّ علـى فسـاد المنهي عنـه في العبـادات والمعاملات خلافًـا للقاضـي أبـي بكر فيهما وفرق فخر الدين بيـن العبادات فيقتضي الفساد وبين المعاملات فلا يقتضي.

First: Prohibition indicates the invalidity (*fasād*) of the prohibited act in both acts of worship (*ʿibādāt*) and transactions (*muʿāmalāt*), contrary to al-Qāḍī Abū Bakr in both.

Fakhr al-Dīn distinguished between acts of worship – where it entails invalidity – and transactions – where it does not entail invalidity.

الثانـي والثالـث: يقتضـي النهي الفـور والتكرار علـى الأصحّ ليحصل الانتهاء من زمان وروده إلى الأبد.

Second and Third: Prohibition entails immediacy and repetition, according to the sounder opinion, so that cessation occurs from the time of its issuance unto perpetuity.

الرابـع: الأمـر يقتضـي النهي عن الأضـداد المأمور بـه كلّها، والنهي يقتضي الأمر بضدّ واحد من أضداد المنهي عنه.

Fourth: The command entails the prohibition of all contraries (*aḍdād*) of the commanded act, while prohibition entails the command of a single contrary among the contraries of the prohibited act

<table>
<tr><td>2.10   ON THE MEANINGS OF
            PARTICLES</td><td>الباب العاشر: في معاني الحروف</td></tr>
</table>

يحتاج إليها الفقيه، وجرت عادة الأُصوليّين بذكرها:

The jurist requires it, and it is the custom of the scholars of *uṣūl* to mention it.

الباء: على ثمانية أنواع: للإلصاق، وهو للتعدّي، وللاستعانة وللقسم، وللمصاحبة، وللتعليل، وزائدة، وظرفيّة، وزاد بعض الكوفيّين للتبعيض.

Bā' has eight types:
1. for adhesion (*ilṣāq*), which is for transitivity (*taʿdiyah*)
2. for seeking assistance (*istiʿānah*)
3. for oath (*qasm*)
4. for accompaniment (*muṣāḥabah*)
5. for causation (*taʿlīl*)
6. superfluous (*zā'idah*)[57]
7. for adverbiality (*ẓarfiyyah*).
some of the Kufans added:
8. for partitivity (*tabʿīḍ*)

اللام: علـى خمسـة أنـواع: للملـك، وللاختصاص، وللاستحقاق، وللتعليل، وللتأكيد وهي المفتوحة.

Lām is of five types:
1. for possession (*milk*)

---

57   (Tr:) In linguistics, referred to as: pleonastic, expletive.

2. for specification (*ikhtiṣāṣ*)
3. for entitlement (*istiḥqāq*)
4. for causation (*taʿlīl*)
5. for emphasis (*taʾkīd*) – and this is the *fatḥah*-bearing form

الـواو: علـى خمسـة أنـواع: واو العطـف، وهي تقتضـي الجمع بين الشـيئين من غير ترتيب في الزمان، وواو الحال، وواو القسـم، وواو ربّ، وواو الناصبة للفعل.

Wāw is of five types:
1. the conjunctive *wāw* (*wāw al-ʿaṭf*), which entails the combination of two things without temporal sequence
2. the circumstantial *wāw* (*wāw al-ḥāl*)
3. the oath *wāw* (*wāw al-qasam*)
4. the *wāw* of *rubba* (*wāw rubba*)
5. the *wāw* that governs the verb in the accusative (*wāw al-nāṣibah lil-fiʿl*)

الفـاء: علـى ثلاثـة أنواع: عاطفة، وفـاء رابطة، وناصبـة للفعل، وهي تقتضي الترتيب، والتسبب، والتعقيب.

Fāʾ is of three types:
1. the coordinating *fāʾ*
2. the connective *fāʾ*
3. the *fāʾ* that governs the verb (*nāṣibah lil-fiʿl*)
And it entails three things:
1. sequence (*tartīb*)
2. causation (*tasabbub*)
3. immediacy (*taʿqīb*)

ثُمَّ: للعطف، وللترتيب، والمهملة.

Thumma [is of three kinds]:
1. for conjunction (*ʿaṭf*)
2. for sequence (*tartīb*)
3. as an unqualified particle (*muhmalah*)

لكن: للاستدراك، ويسمّيها أهل المنطق باستثناء.

Lakin [has one use]: for correction (*istidrāk*), which the logicians call exception (*istithnāʾ*)

حتى: للغاية.

Ḥattā [has one use]: for limit (*ghāyah*)

مِنْ: على أربعة أنواع: للتنويع، ولابتداء الغاية، ولبيان الجنس، وزائدة.

Min is of four types:

1. for classification (*tanwīʿ*)
2. for indicating the starting point of a limit (*ibtidāʾ al-ghāyah*)
3. for specifying the genus (*bayān al-jins*)
4. superfluous (*zāʾidah*)

إلى: لانتهاء الغاية، وقيل بمعنى مع.

Ilā has two meanings:

1. for the termination of a limit (*intihaʾ al-ghāyah*)
2. it is also said to have the same meaning as *maʿ*

الكاف: للتشبيه، والتعليل.

Kāf has two meanings:

1. for similitude (*tashbīh*)
2. for causation (*taʿlīl*)

في: للظرفيّة والسببيّة.

Fī is [for two meanings]:

1. for circumstantiality (*ẓarfiyyah*)
2. for causation (*sababiyyah*)

أو: لها خمسة معان: الشكّ، والإبهام، والتخيير، والإباحة والتنويع.

Aw has five meanings:

1. doubt (*shakk*)
2. ambiguity (*ibhām*)

3. choice (*takhyīr*)
4. permissibility (*ibāḥah*)
5. diversification (*tanwī'*)

إِمَّا: المكسورة المشدّدة، لها أربعة معان: الشكّ، والإبهام، والتخيير، والتنويع.

Immā – the *kasrah*-bearing, *shaddah*-marked form – has four meanings:
1. doubt (*shakk*)
2. ambiguity (*ibhām*)
3. choice (*takhyīr*)
4. classification (*tanwī'*)

أمّا: المفتوحة المشدّدة للتفصيل.

Ammā – the *fatḥah*-bearing, *shaddah*-marked form – is:
1. for specification (*tafsīl*)

أَلَا: للتنبيه، والاستفتاح، وللعرض، والتخصيص.

Alā is [for four uses]:
1. for alerting (*tanbīh*)
2. for initiation (*istiftāḥ*)
3. for offering (*'arḍ*)
4. for specification (*takhsīṣ*)

إنَّ: المكسورة المشدّدة، والمفتوحة المشدّدة، كلاهما للتأكيد.

Inna/Anna – the *kasrah-shaddah* form and the *fatḥah-shaddah* form are both – are for emphasis (*ta'kīd*)

أنْ: المفتوحة المخفّفة، أربعة أنواع: مصدرية، ومخفّفة من الثقيلة، وزائدة، وحرف عبارة وتفسير.

An – the *fatḥah*-bearing, *shaddah*-less form – has four types:
1. infinitival (*maṣdariyyah*)

2. lightened from the heavy (*mukhaffafah min al-thaqīlah*)
3. superfluous (*zāʾidah*)
4. a particle of expression and explanation (*ḥarf ʿibārah wa-tafsīr*)

إنْ: المكسورة المخفّفة، أربعة أنواع: شرطيّة، ونافية، وزائدة، ومخفّفة من الثقيلة.

In – the *kasrah*-bearing, *shaddah*-less form, has four types:
1. conditional (*sharṭiyyah*)
2. negative (*nāfiyah*)
3. superfluous (*zāʾidah*)
4. lightened from the heavy (*mukhaffafah min al-thaqīlah*)

لمَّا: على نوعين: نافية، وحرف وجوب لوجوب.

Lammā is of two types:
1. negative (*nāfiyah*)
2. a particle of necessitation for necessitation (*ḥarf wujūb li-wujūb*)

لوْ: على نوعين: للتمني، ولامتناع شيء لامتناع غيره، وهي للشرطيّة، فإذا دخلت على النفي صيرته إثباتًا، وإن دخلت على الإثبات صيرته نفيًا.

Law is of two kinds:
1. for wishing (*tamannī*)
2. for the impossibility of something due to the impossibility of something else – it is a conditional particle,[58] when it enters upon negation, it renders it affirmation; and when it enters upon affirmation, it renders it negation.

لوْلا: على نوعين: للعرض وللتحضيض، ولامتناع شيء لوجود غيره.

Lawlā is of two kinds: for offering (*ʿarḍ*) and for exhortation (*taḥḍīḍ*); and for the impossibility of a thing due to the existence of another

---

58   (Tr:) A particle introducing the protasis.

3

ON LEGAL RULINGS

الفنّ الثالث من علم الأصول في الأحكام الشرعيّة

وفيه عشرة أبواب:

It comprises ten sections.

<table>
<tr><td>3.1</td><td>ON THE DIVISIONS OF RULINGS</td><td dir="rtl">الباب الأوّل: في أقسام الأحكام</td></tr>
</table>

وهي خمسة: واجب، ومندوب، وحرام، ومكروه ومباح.

They are five: obligatory, recommended, prohibited, reprehensible, and permissible.

فالواجب: ما طلب فعله طلبًا جازمًا.

والمندوب: ما طلب الشرع فعله طلبًا غير جازم.

والمحرّم: ما طلب الشرع تركه طلبًا جازمًا.

والمكروه: ما طلب الشرع تركه طلبًا غير جازم.

والمباح: ما لم يطلب الشرع فعله ولا تركه.

Obligatory (*wājib*) is that whose performance is demanded with decisive demand.

Recommended (*mandūb*) is that which the Law has requested to be performed with a non-decisive request.

Prohibited (*ḥarām*) is that which the Law has demanded be abandoned with a decisive demand.

Reprehensible (*makrūh*) is that which the Law has requested be abandoned, though not with decisive demand.

Permissible (*mubāḥ*) is that which the Law has neither demanded to be done nor to be left.

وهـذه الحـدود صحّ من تحديدها بالثواب والعقاب كقولهم للواجب: ما في فعله ثواب، وفي تركه عقاب لوجهين:

أحدهمـا: إنّ الثـواب والعقاب ليـس أحدهما وصفًا ذاتيًّا للأحكام، وإنّما هما جزاء عليهما، فلا يجوز الحدّ بهما.

والثاني: إنّ العقاب قد يعدم إذا عفا اللَّه، والثواب قد يعدم إذا عدمت النيّة. ومثل ذلك يَرُدُّ على من قال: إنّ الواجب ما ذمّ تاركه، والمحرّم ما ذمّ فاعله.

These definitions are sounder than delimiting by reward and punishment, as in their statement regarding the *obligatory* (*wājib*) as that which, in its performance, there is reward, and in its omission, there is punishment – for two reasons.

First: Reward and punishment are not intrinsic attributes of rulings; rather, they are recompense for them. Therefore, it is not permissible to define rulings by them.

Second: Punishment may be nullified if Allah pardons, and reward may be nullified if intention is absent. The same applies in refutation of one who says: the obligatory is that for which the one who abandons it is reproached, and the prohibited is that for which the one who commits it is reproached.

<table>
<tr><td>3.2</td><td>ON THE NAMES OF THESE DIVISIONS AND THEIR DEGREES</td><td dir="rtl">الباب الثاني: في أسماء هذه الأقسام ودرجاتها</td></tr>
</table>

أمّا الواجـب: فهو الفرض، والمفروض، والمكتوب، والمحتوم، والمستحقّ.

Obligatory (*wājib*) is the *prescribed* (*farḍ*), the *imposed* (*mafrūḍ*), the *written* (*maktūb*), the *decreed* (*maḥtum*), and the *due* (*mustaḥaqq*).

وقالـت الحنفيّـة: الفـرض ما ثبت وجوبه بدليل قطعـيّ، والواجب: ما ثبت وجوبه بدليل مجتهد فيه.

The Ḥanafīs said: The *farḍ* is that whose obligatoriness is established by a definitive proof; the *wājib* is that whose obligatoriness is established by a proof subject to juristic effort (*mujtahad fihi*).

وينقسم الفرض قسمين: فرض عين: وهو ما يجب على كلّ مكلّف، كالصلاة، والصيام، وفرض كفاية: وهو الذي إذا قام به بعض الناس سقط عمـن سـواهم كالصلاة على الجنائز، وطلب العلـم، والجهاد، فإن تواطأ الجميع على تركه أُثِموا.

Prescribed (*farḍ*) is divided into two categories:
1. *Individual prescription (farḍ ʿayn)* – that which is incumbent upon every morally responsible agent, such as prayer and fasting.
2. *Communal prescription (farḍ kifāyah)* – that which, if undertaken by some individuals, is no longer required of the rest – such as the funeral prayer, the pursuit of knowledge, and jihad. If all collectively agree to abandon it, they are all blameworthy.

وأمّا المندوب: فهو المتطوّع، وهو على درجات أعلاها السنّة، ودونها المسـتحبّ، وهـو الفضيلـة ودونهـا النافلة، وقد يقال نافلـة في المندوب على الأعيان وهو الآكد، كالوتر والفجر، وصلاة العيدين، وقد يكون على الكفاية كالآذان والإقامة، وبما يفعل بالأموات من المندوبات.

Recommended (mandūb) is the voluntary act.

It has degrees, the highest of them is the *sunnah*, followed by the *mustaḥabb* – which is virtuous, and below it the *nāfilah*.

The term *nāfilah* may be applied to the *mandūb* that pertains to individuals, and this is the more emphatic, such as the *witr* prayer, the Fajr prayer, and the two ʿĪd prayers.

It may also be communal, such as the *adhān* and the *iqāmah*, and the recommended acts performed for the deceased.

وأمّا الحرام: فهو المُحرَّم والممنوع، والمحظور، والمعصية، والسـيئة، والذنب، والإثم، وهو على درجتين: صغائر وكبائر. وقد يقال فيه مكروه.

Prohibited (ḥarām) is *that which is prohibited (muḥarram), for-bidden (mamnūʿ), proscribed (maḥẓūr), a disobedience (maʿṣiyah), an evil deed (sayyiʾah), a sin (dhanb),* and a *transgression (ithm).*

It is of two degrees: *minor sins (ṣaghāʾir)* and *major sins (kabāʾir)* It may also be referred to as *reprehensible (makrūh).*

وأمّا المكروه: فقد تغلظ كراهيته حتى يقرب من الحرام، وقد تخف.

The *reprehensible:* its reprehensibility may intensify to the point that it approaches the prohibited (*ḥarām*), and it may also lessen.

وأمّـا المبـاح: فهو الـحلال والجائز وقد يعبر عنه بلا جناح، ولا حرج، ولا إثم ولا بأس.

Permissible (mubāḥ) is the *lawful (ḥalāl)* and the *licit (jāʾiz)* and it may also be expressed as: without blame (*bi-lā-junāḥ*), without hardship (*lā ḥaraj*), without sin (*lā ithm*), or without harm (*lā baʾs*).

<table>
<tr><td>3.3</td><td>ON THE EXPANDED
AND DISCRETIONARY
OBLIGATION</td><td>الباب الثالث: في الواجب الموسع والمخيَّر</td></tr>
</table>

ينقسم الواجب بالنظر إلى الوقت قسمين: مضيق وموسّع.

The obligatory act, with respect to time, is divided into two cate-gories: restricted and expanded.

الموسّع: هو أن يكون وقت الفعل يسع أكثر منه، وقد يكون محدودًا كأوقـات الصلـوات، وقـد يكـون غيـر محـدود، بل مُوَسَّعًا بطـول العمر كالحجّ، ويتعلّق الوجوب بجميع الوقت عند جمهور المالكيّة، وقيل بجزء مـن الوقـت غير معيّـن، ويعينه المكلّف بفعله ويعزي إلى الشـافعيّة إنكار

الواجب الموسع، لأنّهم يقولون إنّ الوجوب يتعلّق بأوّل الوقت، ويعزي إلى الحنفيّة إنكاره، لأنّهم يقولون إنّ الوجوب يتعلّق بآخر الوقت.

Expanded obligation (*muwassaʿ*) is the time for the act accommodates more than the act itself. It may be limited, such as the times of the prayers, or it may be unlimited, rather expanded by the length of life, such as the Ḥajj.

According to the majority of the Mālikīs, the obligation pertains to the entirety of the time. It is also said that it pertains to an unspecified part of the time, which is specified by the agent through performance.

Denial of the expanded obligation is attributed to the Shāfiʿīs, for they say that the obligation pertains to the beginning of the time. It is also attributed to the Ḥanafīs, for they say that the obligation pertains to the end of the time.

وأمّا الواجب المخيّر، فمثل كفّارة اليمين، خيّر فيها بين الإطعام والكسوة والعتق، والواجب متعلّق بواحد منها غير معيّن ويُعَيِّنُه المكلّف بفعله، وقالت المعتزلة: الثلاثة كلّها واجبة، وهو اختلاف في عبارة الواجب المرتّب هو الذي لا تجزي الخصلة الثانية منه مع القدرة على الأولى كالعتق والصيام والإطعام في كفّارة الظهار.

Discretionary obligation (*wājib mukhayyar*) is exemplified by the expiation for an oath (*kafārat al-yamīn*), in which there is a choice between feeding, clothing, and manumission. The obligation pertains to one of them, unspecified, and the agent specifies it through his action.

The Muʿtazilah said: All three are obligatory. This is a difference in the expression of the obligation.

The *sequential obligation* (*wājib murattab*) is that in which the second option is not sufficient when the first is possible – such as manumission, fasting, and feeding in the expiation for *ẓihār*.

3.4 ON THE CONDITIONS OF LEGAL RESPONSIBILITY

الباب الرابع: في شروط التكليّف

وهي: العقل، والبلوغ، وحضور الذهـن، وعدم الإكراه، والإسلام، أو بلوغ الدعوة.

They are: the intellect (*ʿaql*), maturity (*bulūgh*), presence of mind, absence of coercion, Islam, and the reaching of the message (*bulūgh al-daʿwah*).

فالعقل: تحرّز من الجمادات والبهائم والمجانين والنائمين.

"The intellect" (*ʿaql*) is a distinguishing feature absent in inanimate objects, animals, the insane, and those asleep.

والبلــوغ: تحــرّز من الصبيان، ولا يعترض علــى هذا بوجوب الزكاة في مال الصبي وغرمه لما أتلف، فإن وليه هو المخاطب بذلك.

"Puberty" (*bulūgh*) is a safeguard from childhood. This is not objectionable by the obligation of almsgiving (*zakāh*) on the wealth of a child and his liability for what he destroys, for it is his guardian who is addressed thereby.

وحضور الذهن: تحرّز من الناسي.

"Presence of mind" is a safeguard from forgetfulness.

واختلف هل يعد عدم الإكراه شــرطًا في التكليّف أم لا؟ والأظهر في مذهب مالك أنّه شرط.

There is a disagreement as to whether the absence of coercion is to be considered a condition for legal responsibility (*taklīf*) or not. The more apparent view in the school of Mālik is that it is a condition.

ولا خلاف أنّ الكفّار مخاطبـون بالإيمـان، واختلـف هـل مخاطبون بفـروع الشــريعة في حـال كفـرهم أم لا؟ فقال قـوم: إنهـم مكلّفون بها

إذا بلغتهم دعوة الرسـول -صلّى اللّه عليه وسـلّم-. وقال قوم: لا يكلّفون بالفروع حتى يُسْلِمُوا، مع الاتّفاق أنّها لا تصح منهم ولا تقبل منهم حتى يؤمنوا، وقال فخر الدين بن الخطيب: «ثمرة الخلاف راجعة إلى مضاعفة العذاب في الآخرة».

There is no disagreement that the disbelievers are addressed with the command to believe. However, there is a difference of opinion as to whether they are addressed with the ancillary rulings (*furūʿ al-sharīʿah*) while in a state of disbelief.

Some have said: They are legally responsible for them once the call of the Messenger – may Allah bless him and give him peace – has reached them.

Others have said: They are not legally responsible for the ancillary rulings until they embrace Islam, while all agree that such acts are neither valid nor accepted from them until they believe.

Fakhr al-Dīn ibn al-Khaṭīb said: "The consequence of the disagreement pertains to the intensification of punishment in the Hereafter."

| 3.5 | ON THE ATTRIBUTES OF ACTS OF WORSHIP | الباب الخامس: في أوصاف العبادات |

وهي ستّة: اثنان متقابلان وهما: الأداء والقضاء، واثنان متقابلان وهما: الصحّة والفساد، واثنان متقابلان وهما: الرخصة والعزيمة.

They are six, in three pairs of opposites: performance and make-up; validity and invalidity; and dispensation and the resolute obligation.

فأمّا الأداء: فهو إيقاع العبادة في وقتها المعيّن لها شرعًا.

والقضاء: إيقاعها بعد وقتها المعيّن لها شرعًا.

Performance (adāʾ) is the enactment of the act of worship within its time specifically designated for it by the Law.

Make-up (qaḍāʾ) is its performance after its time legally appointed.

واختلف هل وجوب القضاء بالأمر الأوّل أو بأمر جديد؟.

There is a disagreement as to whether the obligation to make up a missed act is due to the original command or to a new command.

والعبادات على ثلاث أقسام: منها ما يوصف بالأداء والقضاء كالصلوات الخمس، ومنها ما لا يوصف بها كالنوافل، ومنها ما يوصف بالأداء وحده.

Acts of worship are of three categories: those that are described by both performance and make-up, such as the five daily prayers; those that are not described by either, such as supererogatory acts; and those that are described by performance alone.

وأمّا الصحّة: فهي عند المتكلّمين ما وافق الأمر، وعند الفقهاء ما أسقط القضاء فصلاة من ظنّ الطهارة وهو محدث صحيحة عند المتكلّمين وغير صحيحة عند الفقهاء. وإنّما الخلاف في التسمية لا في الحكم، والصحّة أعمّ من الإجزاء، لأنّ الإجزاء لا يوصف به إلّا الواجب.

Validity (*ṣiḥḥah*), according to the theologians (*mutakallimūn*), is that which accords with the command; and according to the jurists (*fuqahāʾ*) is that which obviates the need for repetition. Thus, the prayer of one who presumed purification while in a state of ritual impurity is valid according to the theologians and invalid according to the jurists.

والفساد نقيض الصحّة: وتكون في العبادات وفي العقود كالبيع والنكاح، وهو أعمّ من البطلان، لأنّ البطلان لا يوصف به إلّا العبادات، وقيل هما مترادفان وهو يوجب الإعادة في الواجب، وعدم ترتيب المقصود في العقود.

The disagreement pertains only to the terminology, not to the ruling. Validity is broader than sufficiency (*ijzāʾ*), for sufficiency is predicated only of that which is obligatory.

Corruption (*fasād*) is the opposite of validity (*ṣiḥḥah*). It occurs in acts of worship and in contracts such as sale and marriage.

It is more general than invalidity (*buṭlān*), for invalidity is only ascribed to acts of worship. It is also said that the two are synonymous.

Corruption necessitates repetition in obligatory acts and the non-realisation of the intended effect in contracts.

وأمّا الرخصة: فهي إباحة فعل المحرّم أو ترك الواجب لسبب اقتضى ذلــك، وقد تنتهــي للوجوب كأكل المضطر الميتةَ، وقد لا تنتهي كإفطار المسافر.

والعزيمة: هي ما لزم العباد من فعل أو ترك.

Dispensation (*rukhṣah*) is the permissibility of performing a prohibited act or omitting an obligatory one due to a cause that necessitates that. It may reach the level of obligation, such as the compelled person eating carrion, or it may not, such as the traveller breaking the fast.

Resolute *obligation* (*ʿazīmah*) is that which is incumbent upon the servants, whether in action or in abstention.

<table>
<tr><td>3.6   ON GOODNESS AND BADNESS</td><td>الباب السادس: في الحسن والقبح</td></tr>
</table>

وهما يطلقان بثلاث إطلاقات:

They are used in three senses.

أحدها: إنّ الحسن ما وافق الطبع أو الغرض والقبيح ما خالفه.

والثاني: إنّ الحسن ما كان صفة كمال والقبح ما كان صفة نقص.

ولا خلاف أنّ الحسن والقبح بهذين الإطلاقين لا يفتقر فيهما إلى ورود شرع.

First: *Goodness* (*ḥasan*) is that which accords with disposition (*ṭabʿ*) or aim (*gharaḍ*); *badness* (*qabīḥ*) is that which opposes it.

Second: *Goodness* is that which is a perfection; *badness* is that which is a deficiency.

There is no disagreement that goodness and badness in these two senses do not depend upon the advent of revealed law (*shar*).

والثالث: إنّ الحسن ما مدحه اللَّه، والقبيح ما ذمّه اللَّه وعاقب عليه، وفي هذا وقع الخلاف، فقال الأشعريّ: إنّه لا يعلم ولا يثبت إلّا بالشرع، وقالت المعتزلة: بل العقل اقتضى ثبوته قبل الرسل صلوات اللَّه عليهم، ولا يفتقر في معرفته إلى شرع، إلّا أنّهم جعلوه ثلاثة أقسام:

١. قسم علمه العقل ضرورة، كحسن الصدق النافع، وقبح الكذب الضار.

٢. وقسم علمه العقل نظرًا، كحسن الصدق الضار والكذب النافع.

٣. وقسم لم يصل إليه العقل، كوجوب صيام آخر يوم من رمضان وتحريم أوّل يوم من شوال.

فالأوّلان ورد الشرع مؤكّدًا لما علمه العقل فيهما، والثالث ورد الشرع فيه مظهرًا لما لم يصل العقل إليه مع أن حسن جميعها وقبحه كان ثابتًا لها قبل الشرع.

Third: *Goodness* is what Allah has praised; *badness* is what Allah has condemned and punished for. On this point, disagreement has arisen.

Al-Ashʿarī said: It is not known nor established except through revealed law (*shar*).

The Mu'tazilah said: Rather, the intellect necessitated its establishment prior to the messengers – may Allah bless them and grant them peace – and knowledge of it does not depend on revealed law. However, they divided it into three categories:

1. a category the intellect knows immediately, such as the goodness of beneficial truthfulness and the evil of harmful falsehood;
2. a category the intellect knows through speculative reasoning, such as the goodness of harmful truthfulness and beneficial falsehood; and
3. a category the intellect does not reach, such as the obligation of fasting on the last day of Ramaḍān and the prohibition of fasting on the first day of Shawwāl.

The first categories two were affirmed by revelation as confirming what the intellect had already known concerning them, and the third was addressed by revelation as disclosing what the intellect had not attained, even though the goodness or badness of all of them was established prior to revelation.

وعند الأشعريّ أنّ الشرع هو الذي أنشأ الحسن أو القبح في الجميع، فإنّه لا يثبت حكم قبل ورود الشرائع.

وقـال الأبهري: الأشـياء قبل ورود الشـرع على المنـع. وقال أبو الفرج على الإباحة وتوقّف غيرهما.

According to al-Ashʿarī, it is revelation that originates the goodness or badness in all cases, for no ruling is established before the advent of the revealed laws.

Abū al-Ḥasan al-Abharī held that things, prior to the coming of revelation, are prohibited.

Abū al-Faraj maintained that they are permitted.

Others withheld judgement.

<table>
<tr><td>3.7</td><td>ON THAT UPON
WHICH RULINGS ARE
DEPENDENT</td><td dir="rtl">الباب السابع: فيما تتوقّف عليه
الأحكام</td></tr>
</table>

وهي ثلاثة: وجود السبب، ووجود الشرط، وانتفاء المانع.

They are three: the existence of the cause, the existence of the condition, and the absence of the impediment.

أمّا السـبب: فهو ما يلزم من وجوده وجود الحكم، ومن عدمه عدمه لذاته كدخول رمضان سبب في وجوب الصوم.

Cause (*sabab*) is that from whose existence the existence of the ruling necessarily follows, and from whose nonexistence its nonexistence necessarily follows in itself – such as the entering of Ramaḍān being a cause for the obligation of fasting.

وأمّا الشـرط: فهو ما يلزم من عدمه عدم الحكم، ولا يلزم من وجوده وجــود الحكم ولا عدمه لذاتـه كالصحّة والإقامة في وجوب الصيام، فإنّ الإنسان قد يكون صحيحًا مقيمًا ولا يجب عليه الصيام في غير رمضان.

Condition (*sharṭ*) is that from whose absence the absence of the ruling necessarily follows, while from its presence the presence or absence of the ruling does not necessarily follow in itself – such as health and residence in the obligation of fasting, for a person may be healthy and resident, yet fasting is not obligatory upon him outside of Ramaḍān.

وأمّــا المانــع: فهو ما يلــزم من وجوده عدم الحكم، ولا يلزم من عدمه وجود الحكم ولا عدمه لذاته كالحيض مع الصيام.

Impediment (*māniʿ*) is that from whose existence the nonexistence of the ruling necessarily follows, while from its nonexistence the existence or nonexistence of the ruling does not necessarily follow in itself – such as menstruation with fasting.

فالمعتبر من المانع وجوده، ومن الشـرط عدمه، ومن السـبب وجوده وعدمه، وإنّما قلنا في كلّ واحد منها «لذاته» تحـرّزًا ممّا يلزم بسبب غيره لتوقّف الحكم على جميعها.

What is operative (*mu'tabar*) in the case of the impediment is its existence; in the case of the condition, its nonexistence; and in the case of the cause, both its existence and its nonexistence.

We have stated "in each of them, on account of its essence," in order to guard against what would follow due to something else, since the ruling depends on all of them.

SUPPLEMENT   تكميل

الشرط المذكور هنا الشرعيّ، فإنّ الشروط على أربعة أقسام:

١. شرعيّة كالطهارة مع الصلاة.

٢. وعقليّة، كالحياة مع العلم.

٣. وعاديّة، كالغذاء مع الحياة في بعض الحيوانات.

٤. ولغويـة، وهـي التـي أدواتها «إنْ» وما في معناهـا، و «لَوْ» و «إذَا». فـ «إنْ» تختصّ بالمشكوك و «إذا» تدخل على المشكوك والمعلوم، و «لو» على الماضي بخلافهما.

The condition mentioned here is the legal one, for conditions are of four kinds:

1. Legal (*shar'ī*), such as purification with prayer.
2. Rational (*'aqlī*), such as life along with knowledge.
3. Habitual (*'ādī*), such as nourishment with life in some animals.
4. Linguistic (*lughawī*), that whose particles are *in*, and those similar in meaning, *law*, and *idhā*.

The particle *in* is specific to the doubtful; *idhā* applies to both the doubtful and the known; and *law* pertains to the past – unlike the other two.

قــال شــهاب الديـن القرافـيّ: «إن للشــروط اللغويّـة أسـباب يلزم من وجودها الوجود، ومن عدمها العدم».

Shihāb al-Dīn al-Qarāfī said: "Linguistic conditions have causes from whose existence the existence [of the conditioned] follows, and from whose absence the non-existence [of the conditioned] follows."

<table>
<tr><td>3.8</td><td>ON THE CATEGORIES OF RIGHTS</td><td>الباب الثامن: في أقسام الحقوق</td></tr>
</table>

وهي ثلاثة:

١. حقّ للّه تعالى فقط كالإيمان والصلاة.

٢. وحقّ للعبد فقط، وهو ما يسقط إذا أسقطه العبد كالديون.

٣. وقسم اختلف هل يغلب فيه حقّ اللَّه، أو حقّ العبد كحدّ القذف.

They [rights (*ḥuqūq*)] are three:

1. A right belonging solely to Allah, such as faith (*īmān*) and prayer.
2. A right belonging solely to the servant, which lapses if the servant relinquishes it, such as debts.
3. A category concerning which there is disagreement as to whether the right of Allah predominates therein or the right of the servant, such as the prescribed punishment (*ḥadd*) of false accusation of fornication (*qadhf*).

<table>
<tr><td>3.9</td><td>ON THE MEANS</td><td>الباب التاسع: في الوسائل</td></tr>
</table>

موارد الأحكام على قسمين: مقاصد ووسائل.

The subjects of rulings are of two kinds: ends and means.

فالمقاصد هي المقصودة لنفسها.

Ends (maqāṣid) are those intended in and of themselves.

والوسائل هي التي توصل إلى المقاصد، فحكمها حكم مقاصدها إذا كانت لا يوصل إليها إلّا بها، فالوسيلة للواجب واجبة كالسعي إلى صلاة الجمعة والوسيلة إلى الحرام حرام، وكذلك سائر الأحكام، وإذا سقط اعتبار المقصد سقط اعتبار الوسيلة.

Means (wasāʾil) are that which lead to the ends; thus, their ruling is the same as that of their ends if the ends cannot be attained except through them. Hence, the means to an obligation are themselves obligatory; such as walking to the Friday prayer; and the means to a prohibition are themselves prohibited, as are all other rulings. When the consideration of the end is nullified, the consideration of the means is likewise nullified.

<table>
<tr><td>3.10   ON THE ACTIONS OF THE MORALLY RESPONSIBLE AGENT CONCERNING EXTERNAL OBJECTS</td><td>الباب العاشر: في تصرفات المكلّفين في الأعيان</td></tr>
</table>

وهي أحد عشر نوعًا:

They are eleven types:

الأوّل: إنشاء ملك في غير مملوك كالاصطياد وإحياء الموات.

First: The origination of ownership in what is unowned, such as hunting and reviving dead land.

الثاني: نقل ملك من ذمّة إلى ذمّة، فقد يكون بعوض كالبيع والإجارة والسلف وبغير عوض كالهبة والصدقة والعمرى والغنيمة.

Second: The transfer of ownership from one liability to another. This may occur:

- with compensation – such as in: sale (*bayʿ*), lease (*ijārah*), and loan (*salf*); or
- without compensation – such as in: gift (*hibah*), charity (*ṣadaqah*), life-grant (*ʿumrā*), and spoils (*ghanimah*).

الثالث: إسقاط حقّ، فقد يكون بعوض كالخلع والعفو عن الجاني على مال وبغير عوض كالعفو لوجه اللّه والعتق.

Third: The relinquishment of a right. This may occur:

- with compensation – such as in: divorce for compensation (*khulʿ*) and pardon of an offender for monetary recompense; or
- without compensation – such as pardon for the sake of Allah and manumission (*ʿitq*).

الرابع: القبض، وهو إمّا بإذن الشارع كاللقطة، أو بإذن غيره كقبض المبيع بإذن البائع، وقبض الرهون وغيرها.

Fourth: Seizure (*qabḍ*). This is either by the permission of the Lawgiver, such as a found item (*luqṭah*); or by the permission of another, such as the seizure of a sold item with the seller's permission, and the seizure of pledges (*rahn*), and the like.

الخامس: الإقباض، وهو الرفع، وقد يكون بالفعل كرفع الثوب إلى مشتريه، أو بالنية فقط، كقبض الوالد وإقباضه من نفسه لولده.

Fifth: Delivery (*iqbāḍ*), which is transfer. It may occur by action, such as lifting a garment to its buyer; or by intention alone, such as the father's taking possession and delivering from himself to his child.

السادس: الالتزام، كالنذور والضمان.

Sixth: Obligation (*iltizām*), such as vows (*nudhūr*), and suretyship (*ḍamān*).

السابع: الخلط، وهي الشركة على اختلاف وجوهها.

Seventh: Commingling (*khalṭ*), which is partnership in its various forms.

الثامن: الاختصاص بالمنافع كإقطاع الأراضين.

Eighth: Exclusive allocation of benefits, such as the granting of lands (*iqṭāʿ*).

التاسع: الإذن، إمّا في الأعيان كالضيافة أو في المنافع كالعارية.

Ninth: Permission (*idhn*), either concerning external objects, such as hospitality; or concerning benefits, such as a loan for use (*ʿāriyah*).

العاشر: الإتلاف، وهو لإصلاح الأجساد كأكل الأطعمة وذبح البهائم أو للدفع، كقتل الحيوان المؤذي أو لحقّ اللّه تعالى كقتل الكفّار وكسر الصلبان، وآلات اللهو.

Tenth: Destruction (*itlāf*), which is:
- for the purpose of restoring bodies, such as eating food and slaughtering animals;
- for repelling harm, such as killing harmful animals; or
- for the right of Allah – exalted is He – such as killing disbelievers and breaking crosses and instruments of diversion.

الحادي عشـر: التأديب والزجر، وهو إمّا مقدّر كالحدود أو غير مقدّر كالتعزير.

Eleventh: Discipline and deterrence (*taʾdīb wa-zajr*), which is either: fixed, such as prescribed punishments (*ḥudūd*); or unfixed, such as discretionary punishment (*taʿzīr*).

4

ON THE EVIDENCES OF RULINGS

الفنّ الرابع من علم الأصول في أدلّة الأحكام

4.1   ON THE ENUMERATION OF THE EVIDENCE

الباب الأوّل : في حصر الأدلّة

وهي على الجملة ثلاثة أنواع : نصّ، ونقل مذهب، واستنباط.

In sum, they are three types [of evidence (*adillah*)]: explicit text, transmitted doctrine, and inference.

فالنصّ : هو الكتاب والسنّة.

ونقل مذهب : هو الإجماع وأقوال الصحابة.

والاستنباط : هو القياس وما أشبهه.

Explicit text (naṣṣ) is the Book and the Sunnah.
Transmitted doctrine (naql madhhab) is consensus (*ijmāʿ*) and the statements of the Companions.
Inference (istinbāṭ) is syllogism (*qiyās*) and what resembles it.[59]

فيجب على العالم أن ينظر المسألة أولًا في الكتاب فإن لم يجدها نظرها في السنّة، فإن لم يجدها نظرها فيما أجمع عليه العلماء أو اختلفوا فيه، فأخذ بالإجماع ورجع بين الأقوال في الخلاف، فإن لم يجدها في

---

59   (Tr:) Note that *qiyās* in the legal sense is analogy (*tamthīl*) while in the logical sense is syllogism.

أقوالهــم اسـتنبط حكمها بالقياس وبغيره من الأدلّـة وعددها على الجملة عشرون ما بين متّفق عليه ومختلف فيه وهي:

It is therefore incumbent upon the scholar to examine the issue first in the Book; if he does not find it therein, he examines it in the Sunnah; if he does not find it therein, he examines it in what the scholars have agreed upon or differed over – taking the consensus and weighing between the opinions in the case of disagreement. If he does not find it in their statements, he derives its ruling by analogy (*qiyās*)[60] and by other evidences, the number of which in general is twenty, comprising both agreed-upon and disputed sources. They are:

(١) الكتاب والسـنّة، وشــرع مـن قبلنا، وإجماع الأمّـة، (٥) وإجماع أهـل المدينـة، وإجمـاع أهـل الكوفـة، وإجمـاع العشـرة مـن الصحابة، وإجمـاع الخلفـاء الأربعة، وقـول الصحابة، (١٠) والقياس والاسـتدلال، والاسـتصحاب، والبراءة الأصليّة، والأخفّ بالأخفّ، (١٥) والاسـتقراء، والاستحسان، والعوائد، والمصلحة، وسدّ الذرائع، (٢٠) والعصمة.

1. the Book (*kitāb*),
2. the Sunnah (*sunnah*),
3. the law of those before us (*shar' man qablana*),
4. the consensus of the community (*ijmā' al-ummah*),
5. the consensus of the people of Medina (*ijmā' ahl al-Madīnah*),
6. the consensus of the people of Kufa (*ijmā' ahl al-Kūfah*),
7. the consensus of the ten Companions (*ijmā' al-'asharah min al-ṣaḥābah*),
8. the consensus of the four caliphs (*ijmā' al-khulafā' al-arba'ah*),
9. the statements of the Companions (*aqwāl al-ṣaḥābah*),
10. analogy (*qiyās*),
11. inferential reasoning (*istidlāl*),

---

60   (Tr:) Here, *qiyās* means the analogy of the jurist and not the syllogism of the logician.

12. presumption of continuity (*istiṣḥāb*),
13. original non-liability (*barāʾah aṣliyyah*),
14. preferring the lighter over the lighter (*al-akhaf bi-l-akhaf*),
15. inductive reasoning (*istiqrāʾ*),
16. juristic preference (*istiḥsān*),
17. customary practice (*ʿawāʾid*),
18. consideration of public interest (*maṣlaḥah*),
19. blocking the means (*sadd al-dharāʾiʿ*),
20. infallibility (*ʿiṣmah*).

4.2 ON THE NOBLE BOOK الباب الثاني: في الكتاب العزيز

وهــو أصــل الأدلّة وأقواها، ونعني به القرآن العظيــم، المكتوب بين دفتي المصحف، المنقول إلينا نقلًا متواترًا بالقراءة المشهورة.

It is the principal and strongest of the evidences. By it is meant the Magnificent Qurʾān, written between the two covers of the codex, transmitted to us through recurrent mass-transmission in the well-known recitation.

فقولنــا: «المكتــوب بين دفتــي المصحف»، لأنّه الــذي اجتمع عليه الصحابة فمن بعدهم وما هو خارج عن ذلك فليس من القرآن.

Our statement "that which is written between the two covers of the codex (*muṣḥaf*)" – because it is that upon which the Companions and those after them agreed, and whatever lies outside of that is not of the Qurʾān.

وقولنــا: «نــقلًا متواتــرًا» تحرّزًا من آيات ليســت في المصحف نقلها الآحــاد ولا يحتــجّ بهــا عند مالك، لأنّها لم تنقــل نقل القرآن من التواتر، ويحتجّ بها عند أبي حنيفة كأخبار الآحاد.

Our statement "by recurrent mass-transmission" is to safeguard against verses not found in the codex, which were transmitted by solitary reports (*āḥād*) and are not admissible as proof according to Mālik, because they were not transmitted with the recurrent mass-transmission of the Qur'ān. However, they are admissible as proof according to Abū Ḥanīfah, like solitary reports (*akhbār al-āḥād*).

وقولنا: «بالقراءة المشـهورة» نعني به القراءات السـبع وما في مثلها أو يقاربهـا فـي الشـهرة وصحّة النقل كقـراءة يعقوب وابـن محيصن وتحرّزنا بذلك من القراءة الشاذّة.

Our statement "by the well-known recitation" refers to the seven canonical recitations[61] and those similar to them or approaching them in fame and soundness of transmission, such as the recitation of Ya'qūb and Ibn Muḥayṣin. By this, we exclude the anomalous (*shādh*) recitation.

ولا يجوز أن يقرأ بحرف إلّا بثلاثة شروط:
أحدها: أن يوافق خطّ المصحف.
والثاني: أن ينقل نقلًا صحيحًا مشهورًا.
والثالث: أن يوافق كلام العرب ولو في بعض اللغات أو بعض الوجوه.

It is not permissible to recite with a variant recitation (*ḥarf*) except under three conditions:

One: That it conform to the script of the codex (*muṣḥaf*).

Second: That it be transmitted through a sound and well-known transmission.

Third: That it accord with the speech of the Arabs, even if in some dialects or some usages.

---

61   (Tr:) The seven canonical recitations in which there is consensus are named after the following *imām*s of recitation: ʿAbdallāh ibn Kathīr al-Dārī al-Makkī (d. 120/737); ʿAbdallāh ibn ʿĀmir al-Yashabī al-Shāmī (d. 118/736); ʿĀṣim ibn Abī al-Najūd al-Asdī al-Kūfī (d. 127/745); Abū ʿAmr Zabbān ibn al-ʿAlāʾ al-Baṣrī (d. 154/770); Ḥamzah ibn Ḥabīb al-Zayyāt al-Kūfī (d. 156/773); Nāfiʿ ibn ʿAbd al-Raḥmān ibn Abī Nuʿaym al-Madanī (d. 169/785); and Abū al-Ḥasan ʿAlī ibn Ḥamzah al-Kisāʾī – the grammarian – al-Kūfī (d. 189/805).

وقد وقع في القرآن ألفاظ من غير لغة كالمشـكاة والإسـتبرق ووقع فيه الحقيقة والمجاز جريًا على منهاج كلام العرب.

There occur in the Qurʾān words from languages other than Arabic, such as *mishkāt* and *istabraq*, and it contains both the literal and the figurative usage, in accordance with the manner of Arab speech.

4.3   ON THE SUNNAH   الباب الثالث: في السُّنَّة

وهي ثلاثة أنواع: قول النبيّ -صلَّى اللَّه عليه وسلَّم- وفعله وإقراره.

It is of three types: the statement of the Prophet (may Allah bless him and grant him peace); his action; and his tacit approval.

[HIS STATEMENT]

فأمَّا قولـه -صلَّى اللَّه عليه وسلَّم- فيحتجّ به كمـا يحتجّ بالقـرآن، لأنَّه -صلَّى اللَّـه عليـه وسلَّم- لا ينطق عن الهـوى، ولقوله تعالـى: ﴿أَطِيعُوا اللَّـهَ وَالرَّسُولَ﴾ [آل عمـران ٣٢]، ويجـري فـيه ما يجري فـي القرآن من المباحث اللغويّة فإنَّها إنَّما تنصرف في الأقوال.

His statement (*qawluhu*) (may Allah bless him and grant him peace) is adduced as proof just as the Qurʾān is adduced as proof, because he (may Allah bless him and grant him peace) does not speak from caprice, and due to His saying, exalted is He: "Obey Allah and the Messenger."[62]

It is subject to the same linguistic inquiries as the Qurʾān, for such inquiries pertain to utterances.

[HIS ACTION]

وأمَّا فعله -صلَّى اللَّه عليه وسلَّم- فينقسم قسمين: قربات وعادات.

---

62   Qurʾān, 3:32.

His action (*fiʿluhu*) (may Allah bless him and grant him peace) is divided into two categories: acts of devotion and customary practices.

فإن كان عادات كالأُكل واللباس والقيام والقعود فهو دليل على الجواز فإتّباعه -صلَّى اللَّه عليه وسلَّم- في كيفيّة ذلك وصفته حسن.

If it [his action] pertains to customary practices such as eating, clothing, standing, and sitting, then it is an indication of permissibility. Thus, following him (may Allah bless him and grant him peace) in the manner and form of that is commendable.

وإن كان من القربات فهو ثلاث أوجه:
أحدهـا: أن يفعلـه بيانًـا لغيره، فحكمه حكم ذلـك المبيّن، فإن بيَّن واجبًا فهو واجب، وإن بيِّن مندوبًا فهو مندوب.
والثاني: أن يفعله امتثالًا لأمر، فحكمه حكم ذلك الأمر من الوجوب والندب.
والثالـث: أن يفعلـه ابتـداءً مـن غيـر سـبب، فاختلـف هـل هو على الوجوب أو الندب؟.

If it [his action] is among the acts of devotion, then it has three aspects:

First: That he performs it as a clarification of something else; its ruling follows the ruling of that which is clarified, hence: if he clarifies something obligatory, then it is obligatory; and if he clarifies something recommended, then it is recommended.

Second: That he performs it in compliance with a command; its ruling follows the ruling of that command, whether obligation or recommendation.

Third: That he performs it initially without a cause. There is a disagreement as to whether it is obligatory or recommended.

BRANCHES

فروع

الأوّل: إذا ثبت حكم في حقه -صلّى اللَّه عليه وسلّم- ثبت في حقّ أمّته إلّا أن يدلّ دليل على تخصيص ذلك به.

First: If a ruling is established with respect to him (may Allah bless him and grant him peace) it is established with respect to his community, unless there is evidence indicating that it is specific to him.

الثاني: يقع بفعله -صلّى اللَّه عليه وسلّم- جميع أنواع البيان من بيان المجمل، وتخصيص العموم وتأويل الظاهر والنسخ.

Second: All types of clarification[63] occur through his (may Allah bless him and grant him peace) action, including: clarification of the ambiguous, specification of the general, interpretation of the apparent, and abrogation.

الثالث: إذا تعارض قوله -صلّى اللَّه عليه وسلّم- وفعله، فاختلف هل يرجّح القول أو الفعل والأرجح ترجيح القول لأنّه يدلّ بصيغته، وهذا إذا لم يعلم التاريخ فإن علم نسخ المتأخّر المتقدّم.

Third: If his (may Allah bless him and grant him peace) saying and action conflict, there is a difference of opinion as to whether the saying or the action is to be given precedence. The more correct view is that the saying is to be given preferential weighing (*tarjīh*), because it indicates by its formulation. This applies when the chronology is unknown; but if it is known, then the later abrogates the earlier.

[HIS TACIT APPROVAL]

وأمّا إقراره -صلّى اللَّه عليه وسلّم- فهو أن يسمع شيئًا فلا ينكره أو يرى فعلًا فلا ينكره مع عدم الموانع، فيدلّ ذلك على جوازه، وأمّا ما فعل في

---

63   See §2.6.2.

زمانـه فلـم ينكـره، فإن كان ممّـا لا يجوز في العـادة أن يخفي عليه فهو كإقراره، وإن كان ممّا يجوز أن يخفي عليه فلا حجّة فيه.

His *tacit approval* (*taqrīr*) (may Allah bless him and grant him peace) is that he hears something and does not disapprove of it, or sees an action and does not disapprove of it, in the absence of any impediments (*mawāni'*). This indicates its permissibility.

What was done during his time and he did not disapprove of it: if it is of the kind that customarily could not have been hidden from him, then it is like his approval; but if it is of the kind that could have been hidden from him, then it is not a valid proof.

APPENDIX   إلحاق

يناسـب هذا الفصل شـرع من قبلنا من الأنبياء عليهم السلام، واختلف هل شرع لنا أم لا؟ على ثلاثة أقوال:

أحدها: أنّ شرعَ جميعهم شرعٌ لنا.

والثاني: أنّ شرعَ جميعهم ليس شرعًا لنا.

والثالث: التفرقة بين إبراهيم الخليل عليه السلام وغيره، فيكون شـرعُه شرعًا لنا بخلاف غيره.

This section accords with the law of those who came before us (*shar' man qabluna*) from among the prophets – peace be upon them. There is a difference of opinion as to whether it is legislated for us or not, with three views:

First: That the law of all of them is a law for us.

Second: That the law of all of them is not a law for us.

Third: The distinction between Ibrāhīm al-Khalīl (the Friend) – peace be upon him – and others, such that his law is a law for us, unlike that of others.

وهذه الأقوال إنّما هي في المسـائل التي لم يثبت حكمها في شـرعنا فأمّـا ثبـت في شـرعنا فهو على ما ثبت فيه سـواء وافق شـرع مـن قبلنا أو خالفه .

These statements pertain only to issues whose rulings have not been established in our revealed law. What has been established in our revealed law remains as it has been established therein, whether it accords with the law of those before us or differs from it.

4.4 ON REPORTS الباب الرابع: في الخبر

وهـو الكلام المحتمل للتصديـق والتكذيب، وهذه العبارة أولى ممّن قال الصدق والكذب لأنّ خبر اللَّه ورسوله -صلّى اللَّه عليه وسلّم- لا يحتمل إلّا الصدق وخبر الكاذب كمسيلمة لا يحتمل إلّا الكذب .

وفائدة هذا الباب معرفة نقل السنّة، وفيه ثلاثة فصول:

It [report (*khabar*)] is speech that admits of affirmation and denial. This formulation is preferable to that of one who says "[admits of] truth and falsehood," because the report of Allah and His Messenger (may Allah bless him and grant him peace) admits only of truth, while the report of a liar, such as Musaylimah, admits only of falsehood.

The benefit of this chapter lies in knowledge of the transmission of the Sunnah, and it comprises three sections.

4.4.1 ON RECURRENT MASS-TRANSMISSION الفصل الأوّل: في التواتر

نقل الخبر على نوعين: متواتر، ونقل أُحاد .

Transmission of reports is of two kinds: recurrent mass-transmission and solitary transmission.

فأمّـا التواتـر فهو خبر ينقله جماعة يسـتحيل في العــادة تواطؤهم على الكذب. قال فخر الدين بن الخطيـب: «إنَّ عددهم غير محصور، خلافًا لمن حصرهم في اثنتي عشـر أو في أربعين أو سـبعين أو ثلاثمائة أو غير ذلك والأربعة ليست منه عند الجمهور» وعلى أنّه قد قال ابن حزم: «إنّ نقل الاثنين العدلين يوجب العلم».

Recurrent mass-transmission (*tawātur*) is a report transmitted by a group whose collusion upon falsehood is customarily impossible.

Fakhr al-Dīn ibn al-Khaṭīb said their number is not fixed – contrary to those who restricted it to twelve, or to forty, or to seventy, or to three hundred, or to other such numbers. Four transmitters are not sufficient for it, according to the majority.

Ibn Ḥazm said the transmission of two upright individuals yields knowledge.

والتواتر يفيد العلم بشرطين:

أحدهما: أن يستوي طرفاه وواسطته في كثرة الناقلين.

والآخر: أن يكون مستندًا إلى أمر معلوم بالحسّ تحرّزًا من الظنون ومن المعلوم بالنظر.

Recurrent mass-transmission yields knowledge on two conditions:

First: That its two ends and its middle be equal in the number of transmitters.[64]

Second: That it be grounded in something known by sensation, as a safeguard against presumptions and against what is known speculatively (*naẓarī*).

---

64   (Tr:) Meaning that they meet the conditions for *tawātur*, not that each level have the same number of transmitters.

NOTE

تنبيه

يحصـــل العلـــم بالخبـــر بطرق غيـــر التواتر، وهـــي كون المخبر عنــه معلومًا بالضرورة، أو بالاستدلال، أو خبر رسوله -صلّى اللّه عليه وسلّم-، أو خبر مجموع الأمّة، أو القرائن عند أبي المعالي وأبي حامد.

Knowledge through reports (*khabar*) is attained by means other than recurrent mass-transmission, namely: the reported matter being known by necessity (*ḍarūrah*); through inferential reasoning (*istidlāl*); through the report of the Messenger (may Allah bless him and grant him peace); through the report of the entirety of the community; or through contextual indicators, according to Abū al-Maʿālī and Abū Ḥāmid.

الفصل الثاني: في أخبار الآحاد   4.4.2 ON SOLITARY REPORTS

وأمّا نقل الآحاد فهو خبر الواحد أو الجماعة الذين لا يبلغون حدّ التواتر، وهو لا يفيد العلم وإنّما يفيد الظنّ، وهو حجّة عند مالك وغيره بشروط.

Solitary report (*khabar al-āḥād*) is the report of a single individual or of a group that does not reach the level of recurrent mass-transmission.

It does not yield knowledge but rather yields presumption.

It is authoritative according to Mālik and others, with conditions.

منها: أن يكون الراوي حين السماع مميّزًا سواء كان بالغًا أو غير بالغ.

Among the conditions is that the transmitter, at the time of hearing, be discerning (*mumayyiz*), whether having reached legal majority (*bulūgh*) or not.

وأن يكـون عنـد التحديـث عـاقلًا بالغًا مسـلمًا عـدلًا، والعدالة هـي اجتنـاب الكبائر وتوقي الصغائر واجتناب المباحات القادحة في المروءة،

والصحابـة كلّهـم عدول وتثبت العدالـة بالاختبار أو التزكية، واختلف هل يكفي في التعديل والتجريح واحد أم لا؟

وتقبل رواية الفاسق ومجهول الحال، واختلفوا في قبول رواية المبتدع.

[Among the conditions:] that at the time of transmission he be rational (*'āqil*), mature (*bāligh*), Muslim, and upright (*'adl*).

Uprightness (*'adālah*) is the avoidance of major sins, caution regarding minor sins, and refraining from permissible acts that compromise moral integrity (*murū'ah*).

All of the Companions are upright.

Uprightness is established through testing or through commendation.

There is a disagreement as to whether one person suffices for validation or discreditation, or not.

The narration of the transgressor and the one of unknown state (*majhūl al-ḥāl*) is accepted.

They differed concerning the acceptance of the narration of the innovator (*mubtadi'*).

ومنها أن يكون الراوي فقيهًا اشترطه مالك خلافًا لغيره.

Among the conditions is that the transmitter be a jurist; Mālik stipulated this, contrary to others.

ومنهـا أن لا يثبـت كذب الخبر لمخالفتـه لما علم بالتواتر أو الضرورة أو الدليل القاطع، أو أن يكون شأنه أن يتواتر ولم يتواتر.

Among the conditions is that the falsehood of the report is not established due to its contradiction with what is known by recurrent mass-transmission, or by immediate knowledge, or by a definitive proof; or that its nature is such that it ought to have been recurrently mass-transmitted but was not.

ولا يقدح في الرواية تساهل الـراوي في غيـر الحديـث، ولا جهله بالعربيّة، ولا مخالفة الناس لروايته، ولا كون مذهب على خلاف روايته.

The reliability of a narration is not undermined by the narrator's leniency in matters other than ḥadīth, nor by his ignorance of Arabic, nor by others' disagreement with his narration, nor by the fact that his school of thought is contrary to his narration.

4.4.3 ON THE EXAMINATION OF THE MANNER OF TRANSMISSION AND THE NARRATOR'S PHRASING

الفصل الثالث: في النظر في كيفيّة الرواية وألفاظ الراوي

أمّـا كيفيّـة الرواية فسـتّ مراتب، أعلاها السـماع من الشـيخ، ثمّ القراءة عليـه ثمّ السـماع عليه، ثـمّ المناولة، ثمّ الإجازة بالمشـافهة، ثمّ الإجازة بالمكاتبة.

The modes of transmission are six ranks, the highest of which is hearing from the shaykh [the transmitter], then reading to him, then hearing in his presence, then hand-to-hand transmission (*munāwala*), then oral authorisation (*ijāzah bi-l-mushāfahah*), and then written authorisation (*ijāzah bi-l-mukātabah*).

وأمّا ألفاظ الراوي، فإن كان من الصحابة فألفاظه ستّ مراتب:

The transmitter's expressions from one of the Companions fall into six ranks.

الأوّل: أن يقول «سـمعت رسـول اللَّه -صلّى اللَّه عليه وسلّم- يقول»، أو «حدّثنـي» أو «أخبرنـي» أو «قـال لي»، فهذا نصّ في تلقّيه لذلك من رسول اللَّه -صلّى اللَّه عليه وسلّم-.

First: That he says: "I heard the Messenger of Allah (may Allah bless him and grant him peace) say," "He narrated to me" (*ḥaddathanī*), "He informed me" (*akhbaranī*), or "He said to me" (*qāla lī*).

This is explicit text indicating that he received it from the Messenger of Allah – may Allah bless him and grant him peace.

أو «أخبـر» أو «حـدّث»، وهذه ظاهرة في التلقّي منه -صلّى اللَّه عليه وسلّم- وعلى ذلك يحمل وليس نصًّا.

[**Second:**] That he says: "He informed" (*akhbara*) or "He narrated" (*ḥaddatha*).

This indicates reception from him (may Allah bless him and grant him peace) and it is to be construed accordingly, though it is not explicit.

ومثلـه «أمـر رسـول اللَّه -صلّى اللَّه عليه وسلّم- بكـذا» أو «نهى عن كذا»، فهذه محتملة هل سمعه منه أم لا؟

[**Third:**] Likewise is [that he says]: "The Messenger of Allah (may Allah bless him and grant him peace) commanded such-and-such," or "He forbade such-and-such."

It is indeterminate whether he heard it from him or not.

الرابعـة: أن يقـول «أمرنا بكـذا» أو «نهينا عن كذا»، فيتطرّق إلى هذا احتمـال ثانٍ وهـو هل أمر به رسـول اللَّه -صلّى اللَّه عليه وسلّم- أو غيره إلّا أن قالها أبو بكر الصديق فيعلم أنّه لم يأتمر عليه أحد غير رسول اللَّه -صلّى اللَّه عليه وسلّم-.

Fourth: That he says: "We were commanded with such-and-such," or "We were prohibited from such-and-such."

A second possibility then arises concerning this – namely, whether the Messenger of Allah (may Allah bless him and grant him peace) commanded it, or someone else. However, if it was said by Abū Bakr al-Ṣiddīq, it is known that no one other than the Messenger of Allah (may Allah bless him and grant him peace) commanded him.

الخامسـة: أن يقـول «كنا نفعل كـذا»، فيتطرّق إليه احتمال هل كان

في زمان النبيّ -صلّى اللَّه عليه وسلّم- أم لا.

Fifth: That he says: "We used to do such-and-such," which introduces the possibility of whether it was during the time of the Prophet (may Allah bless him and grant him peace) or not.

وإذا قال غير الصحابيّ «قال رسول اللَّه -صلّى اللَّه عليه وسلّم-» فهذا

مرسل، وهو حجّة عند مالك وأبي حنيفة خلافًا للشافعيّ.

And if someone other than a Companion says: "The Messenger of Allah (may Allah bless him and grant him peace) said," then this is a *mursal* (sent report). It is a proof according to Mālik and Abū Ḥanīfah, contrary to al-Shāfiʿī.

واختلف هل ينقل الحديث بالمعنى، واشترط الذين أجازوه أن لا يزيد

في المعنى ولا ينقص ولا يكون أخفى.

There is a disagreement regarding whether a ḥadīth may be transmitted by meaning. Those who permitted it stipulated that the meaning must not be increased, diminished, or rendered more obscure.

وأمّا ألفاظ غير الصحابيّ فعلى أربع مراتب:

الأولى: «حدّثني» أو «أخبرني» أو «سمعته».

الثانية: أن يقال له «أسمعت هذا؟» فيقول «نعم».

الثالثة: أن يقال له «أسمعت هذا؟» فيشير بإصبعه أو برأسه.

الرابعة: أن يقرأ عليه ولا ينكر ولا يتعرّف بإشارة ولا غيرها.

The expressions of one other than a Companion fall into four ranks:
First: "He narrated to me" (*ḥaddathanī*), "He informed me" (*akhbaranī*), or "I heard him" (*samiʿtuhu*).

Second: That it be said to him, "Did you hear this?" and he replies, "Yes."

Third: That he be asked, "Did you hear this?" and he gestures with his finger or his head.

Fourth: That it be recited to him, and he neither reject it nor indicate recognition, whether by gesture or otherwise.

4.5   ON ABROGATION   الباب الخامس: في النسخ

وهو يتطرّق إلى الكتاب والسنّة دون غيرهما، فلذلك ذكرناه عقبهما، وفيه ثلاثة فصول:

It [*abrogation* (*naskh*)] pertains exclusively to the Book and the Sunnah, and for that reason we mentioned it after them. It comprises three sections.

4.5.1   ON ITS REALITY   الفصل الأوّل: في حقيقته

ومعناه لغـةً: الإزالة كقولهم «نسـخت الشـمس الظلّ»، والنقل كنسـخ الكتـاب وحده شـرعًا: الخطاب الدالّ علـى ارتفاع حكم ثابت بخطاب متقدّم مع تراخيه عنه.

Its linguistic meaning is removal (*izālah*), as in their saying, "The sun effaced (*nasakhat*) the shadow," and transference (*naql*), as in the copying (*nasakh*) of a book.

Its technical meaning in the Sharīʿah is the discourse indicating the abrogation of a ruling established by a preceding discourse, with a delay from it.

والفرق بينه وبين التخصيص من ثلاثة أوجه:

الأوّل: أنّ النسخ بعد ثبوت الحكم بخلاف التخصيص.

الثاني: أنّ النسخ متراخٍ عن المنسوخ، والتخصيص قد يكون متراخيًا ومتّصلًا.

الثالث: أنّ النسخ إبطال الجميع والتخصيص إخراج البعض.

The difference between abrogation (*naskh*) and specification (*takhṣīṣ*) is in three respects:

First: Abrogation occurs after the establishment of the ruling, unlike specification.

Second: Abrogation is subsequent to the abrogated, whereas specification may be either subsequent or immediate.

Third: Abrogation is the nullification of the whole, whereas specification is the exclusion of a part.

4.5.2 ON ITS RULING الفصل الثاني: في حكمه

والنسخ جائز عقلًا وواقع شرعًا، وأنكره اليهود لعنهم اللَّه وقالوا يلزم منه البداء وهو محال على اللَّه، وقولهم باطل، والدليل على بطلانه من ثلاثة أوجه:

Abrogation (*naskh*) is rationally possible and has occurred according to the Law.

الأوّل: ما اتّفقت عليه الأمم من نكاح الأخوات غير التوأمة في زمان آدم، ثمّ تحريمه في جميع الملل.

الثاني: أنّ اليهود وافقوا على أنّ شريعتهم نسخت ما قبلها، فلمّا جاز ذلك يجوز أن ينسخها ما بعدها.

الثالث: الفرق بين النسخ والبداء هو أن يظهر له ما كان خفيًّا عليه، والنسخ ليس كذلك، إنّما هو كتحديد مدّة للحكم مثل أن يأمر السيّد عبده بعمل فإذا بلغ منه المقدار الذي أراد السيّد، رفع يده عنه وأمر بعمل آخر.

The Jews – may Allah curse them – denied it, claiming that it entails alteration of the divine will (*badā'*), which is impossible for Allah. Their claim is false, and the proof of its falsehood is from three aspects:

First: That upon which the nations agreed – marriage to non-twin sisters in the time of Ādam [(peace be upon him)], then its prohibition in all religious communities.

Second: The Jews agreed that their law abrogated what preceded it; therefore, if that was possible, it is likewise possible for what comes after it to abrogate it.

Third: The difference between abrogation (*naskh*) and alteration of divine will (*badā'*) is that in the latter, something becomes manifest to Him that was previously hidden from Him, whereas abrogation is not so. Rather, it is like specifying a duration for a ruling – such as when a master commands his servant to perform a task, and once the servant reaches the extent intended by the master, the master withdraws the command and issues a new one.

[ITS CONDITIONS]

ولا يجوز النسخ إلّا بثلاثة شروط:

Abrogation is not possible except under three conditions:

أحدهــا: أن يكــون في الأحكام لا في الاعتقادات ولا في الأخبار إلّا إذا اقتضت حكمًا.

First: That it pertains to rulings, not to beliefs nor to reports – except when a report entails a ruling.

والثاني: أن يكون في الكتاب والسنّة، لأنّ الإجماع والقياس لا ينسخ واحد منهما ولا ينسخ.

Second: That it be in the Book and the Sunnah, for consensus (*ijmā'*) and analogical reasoning (*qiyās*) neither abrogate either of them nor are abrogated.

والثالـث : أن يكـون الناسـخ متأخّرًا والمنسـوخ متقدّمًـا، ويعرف ذلك بالنـصّ علـى التأخيـر أو معرفة وقتهما أو برواية من مات قبل رواية الحكم الآخر.

ويعـرف النسـخ بالنصّ على الرفع أو على ثبـوت النقيض أو بالضدّ أو بإجماع الأمّة على النسخ.

Third: That the abrogating (*nāsikh*) is subsequent and the abrogated (*mansūkh*) is antecedent. This is known by an explicit statement indicating the delay, knowledge of their respective times, or a narration from one who died before the narration of the other ruling.

Abrogation is known by a text explicitly indicating abrogation, a text affirming the establishment of the contradictory, a text affirming the contrary, or the consensus (*ijmāʿ*) of the community on the abrogation.

4.5.3 ON THE ABROGATING AND THE ABROGATED

لفصل الثالث: في الناسخ والمنسوخ

أمّا القرآن فينسـخ بالقرآن، واختلف في نسـخه بالسـنّة المتواترة ولا ينسخ بأخبار الآحاد خلافًا للقاضي أبي الوليد وبعض أهل الظاهر.

The Qurʾān is abrogated by the Qurʾān.

There is disagreement regarding its abrogation by recurrent mass-transmitted Sunnah, and it is not abrogated by solitary reports, contrary to the opinion of Qāḍī Abū al-Walīd and some of the Ẓāhiriyyah.

أمّا السنّة المتواترة فتنسخ بالقرآن أو بالسنّة المتواترة لا بالآحاد.

The recurrent mass-transmitted Sunnah is abrogated by the Qurʾān or by recurrent mass-transmitted Sunnah, not by solitary reports.

وَأمّا أخبار الآحاد فتنسخ بالقرآن أو بالسنّة المتواترة أو بالآحاد.

Solitary reports may be abrogated by the Qur'ān, by recurrent mass-transmitted Sunnah, or by solitary reports.

ويجوز نسخ الأثقل بالأخفّ وعكسه، والنسخ بالمثل والنسخ إلى غير بدل.

Abrogation of what is more burdensome by what is lighter, and its converse, is possible, as is abrogation by an equivalent and abrogation without a substitute.

والمنسوخ بالقرآن على ثلاثة أنواع: منسوخ التلاوة والحكم، ومنسوخ التلاوة دون الحكم، ومنسوخ الحكم دون التلاوة.

That which is abrogated by the Qur'ān is of three types: that whose recitation and ruling are both abrogated; that whose recitation is abrogated but not its ruling; and that whose ruling is abrogated but not its recitation.

4.6 ON CONSENSUS	الباب السادس: في الإجماع

وفيه فصلان:

It comprises two sections.

4.6.1 ON THE CONSENSUS OF THE UMMAH	الفصل الأوّل: في إجماع الأمّة

وهو اتّفاق العُلماء على حكم شرعيّ وهو حجّة عند جمهور الأمّة خلافًا للخوارج والروافض، وإجماع كلّ عصر حجّة لا يشترط الأمّة إلى يوم القيامة لانتفاء فائدة الإجماع، ولا يشترط انقراض العصر خلافًا لقوم.

It [*consensus (ijmāʿ)*] is the agreement of the scholars on a legal ruling.

It is authoritative according to the majority of the community (*ummah*), contrary to the Khārijites and the Rāfiḍites.

The consensus of each era is authoritative.

It is not a condition that the entire community agree until the Day of Resurrection, for that would nullify the benefit of consensus.

Nor is the passing of the era a condition, contrary to the view of some.

وقــال داود الظاهـريّ: إجمـــاع غيــر الصحابــة ليس بحجّـة، ولا يعتبر إجمـــاع العوام خلافًا للقاضي أبي بكر. والمعتبر في كلّ فنّ إجماع أهله وإن لم يكونوا من غير أهله ولا يعتبر منهم إلّا المجتهدون لا المقلّدون.

Dāwūd al-Ẓāhirī said: The consensus of those other than the Companions is not authoritative, and the consensus of the commoners is not to be considered – contrary to the view of al-Qāḍī Abū Bakr.

What is to be considered in every discipline is the consensus of its specialists, even if they are not specialists in other disciplines. Only the independent jurists (*mujtahidūn*) among them are to be considered, not the unqualified followers of authority (*muqallidūn*).

BRANCHES　　　　　　　　　　　　　　　　　　　　　　فروع

الأوّل: يجوز حصول الاتّفاق بعد الاختلاف في العصر الواحد وفي العصر الثاني.

First: It is possible for agreement to occur after disagreement, whether in the same era or in a subsequent era.

الثاني: إذا اختلف أهل العصر الأوّل على قولين فلا يجوز لمَن بعدهم إحداث قول ثالث خلافًا للظاهريّة.

Second: If the people of the first era disagreed over two positions, it is not permissible for those who come after them to introduce a third position – contrary to the Ẓāhiriyyah.

الثالـث: إذا حكـم بعـض الأُمّـة وسـكت الباقون فهو حجّـة وإجماع ويُسمّى الإجماع السكوتيّ، وقيل هو حجّة وليس بإجماع.

Third: If some of the community issue a ruling and the rest remain silent, it is a proof and a consensus, and is called silent consensus (*ijmā' sukūtī*).

It is also said that it is a proof but not a consensus.

الرابع: يجوز عند مالك انعقاد الإجماع عن الدليل والأمارة والقياس.

Fourth: According to Mālik, consensus may be validly constituted on the basis of a proof (*dalīl*), an indicator (*amārah*), or analogical reasoning (*qiyās*).

الخامس: إذا نقل الإجماع بأخبار الآحاد فقيل هو حجّة وقيل لا.

Fifth: If consensus is transmitted by solitary reports (*akhbār āḥād*), it is said to be a probative proof (*ḥujjah*), and it is said not to be.

<table><tr><td>

4.6.2 ON THE REMAINING TYPES
OF CONSENSUS
</td><td>

الفصل الثاني: في بقية أنواع الإجماع
</td></tr></table>

أمّا إجماع أهل المدينة فهو حجّة عند مالك وأصحابه وهو عندهم مقدّم على الأخبار خلافًا لسائر العلماء، وهو من وجوه الترجيح عند الجميع.

The consensus of the people of Medina is a probative proof according to Mālik and his companions; in their view, it is given precedence (*muqaddam*) over reports – contrary to the rest of the scholars.

It is one of the modes of preferential weighing (*tarjīḥ*) according to all.

وأمّـا إجمـاع أهل الكوفة فقال به قـوم لكثرة من دخلها من الصحابة، وكذلك قال قوم بإجماع العترة وبإجماع الخلفاء الأربعة لفضلهم.

Some have upheld the consensus of the people of Kūfah due to the large number of Companions who entered it.

Likewise, some have upheld the consensus of the Prophet's family (*ʿitrah*) and the consensus of the four caliphs due to their merit.

وأمّا قول الصحابيّ إذا لم يكن له مخالف، فإن انتشر ذلك القول في الصحابة فهو حجّة كالإجماع السكوتيّ، وإن لم ينتشر فمذهب مالك أنّه حجّة، واختلف فيه قول الشافعيّ.

وأمّا إذا اختلف الصحابة على قولين فهما دليلان تعارضا فيرجّح أحدهما بكثرة العدد أو بموافقة أحد الخلفاء الأربعة عليه، وإن استويا وجب الرجوع إلى دليل آخر.

If the statement of a Companion has no opposing view, then if that statement became widespread among the Companions, it is a proof, like silent consensus (*ijmāʿ sukūtī*). But if it did not become widespread, then according to the school of Mālik it is a probative proof, while al-Shāfiʿī had differing views on it.

When the Companions differed into two opinions, then both are evidences that have come into conflict, so one of them is given preference either due to the greater number of adherents or due to the agreement of one of the four caliphs with it. If they are equal, it becomes obligatory to refer to another evidence.

4.7   ON ANALOGY   الباب السابع: في القياس

وهو أكمل الرأي ومجال الاجتهاد، وبه تثبت أكثر الأحكام، فإنّ نصوص الكتاب والسنّة محصورة، ومواضع الإجماع معدودة، والوقائع غير محصورة، فاضطرّ العلماء إلى أن يثبتوا منها بالقياس لعالم يثبت بنصّ ولا إجماع.

It [analogy (*qiyās*)] is the most complete opinion and the domain of *ijtihād* (independent juristic reasoning), and most rulings are established by it. For the texts of the Book and the Sunnah are limited, the instances of consensus are enumerated, while occurrences are innumerable. Thus, the scholars were compelled to establish by analogy what is not established by text or consensus.

والقيـاس حجّـة عنـد العلماء من الصحابة فمن بعدهـم إلّا الظاهريّة، ونتكلّم في حدّه ومواضعه، وشروطه، وأنواعه، ومفسراته:

Analogy is a valid probative proof according to the scholars from among the Companions and those after them, except the Ẓāhiriyyah.

We shall discuss its definition, its loci, its conditions, its types, and its invalidators.

4.7.1   ON ITS DEFINITION AND   الفصل الأوّل: في حدّه ومواضعه
        LOCATIONS

أمّـا حـدّه فهـو: «حمل معلـوم على معلوم في إثبات حكـم لهما أو نفيه عنهما بأمر جامع بينهما».

Its definition is that it [*analogy* (*qiyās*)] is the construing of one known (*maʿlūm*) upon another, in affirming or negating a ruling for them both, by means of a unifying factor between them.

فقولنا: «معلوم» نعني به الاشـتراك بين المعلوم والمظنون، ويدخـل فيه أيضًـا الموجـود والمعـدوم، وأوجز من ذلك أن تقـول القياس: «هو إثبات حكـم المنطـوق به للمسـكوت عنـه لجامـع بينهما»، فالمنطـوق به هو المقيس عليه وهو الأصـل، والمسكوت عنه هو المقيس وهو الفرع.

Our statement "known" (*maʿlūm*) denotes the commonality between what is known and what is presumed (*maẓnūn*), and it also includes both what possesses ontological actuality (*mawjūd*) and what is non-actual (*maʿdūm*).

More concisely, one may say that *analogy* (*qiyās*) is the ascription of the ruling of the stated case to the unstated case due to a commonality between them.

The stated case is the case upon which analogy is made (*maqīs ʿalayh*) – the original case (*aṣl*) – and the unstated case is the case analogised (*maqīs*) – the derivative case (*farʿ*).

وأمّا مواضعه فيدخل في الأحكام الشرعيّة وهو مقصودنا، وفي الأحكام العقليّة، وفي الأحكام اللغويّة.

As for its loci, it enters into: legal rulings, which is our intended subject; rational rulings; and linguistic rulings.

ولا يدخل في الأسباب مثل أن يقول في طلوع الشـمس أنّه موجب للصلاة كغروبها، ويدخل في المقدرات كالكفّارات خلافًا لأبي حنيفة.

It does not enter into causes (*asbāb*), such as saying that the rising of the sun necessitates prayer as does its setting. However, it does enter into fixed quantifications (*muqadarrat*), such as expiations, contrary to Abū Ḥanīfah.

ولا يجوز القياس على الرخص خلافًا للشافعيّ.

Analogy may not be made on dispensations, contrary to al-Shāfiʿī.

　　　　الفصل الثاني: في شروطه

وهي ثمانية منها ما يشترط في الأصل والفرع:

They are eight, among which are those conditions required of both the original case and the derivative:

الأوّل: أن يكون حكم الأصل شرعيًّا.

الثاني: أن يثبت بدليل شرعيّ.

الثالث: أن يكون ثابتًا غير منسوخ.

الرابع: أن يكون متّفقًا عليه عند جميع العلماء أو عند الخصمين.

First: That the [type of] ruling of the principal case be legal (*sharī*).
Second: That it be established by a revealed proof.
Third: That it be established and not abrogated.
Fourth: That it be agreed upon by all scholars or by both disputants.

الخامس: أن لا يكون الأصل فرعًا لأصل آخر، وفي هذا خلاف.

السادس: أن لا يخرج الأصل عن باب القياس كالتعبّدات من عدد ركعات الصلاة ومقادير الحدود وشبه ذلك، وما اختصّ به النبيّ -صلّى الله عليه وسلّم- من الأحكام.

السابع: أن يكون الوصف الجامع موجودًا في الفرع كما هو في الأصل.

الثامن: أن لا يكون الفرع منصوصًا فإنّ القياس لا يعتبر مع وجود النصّ.

Fifth: That the original case not be a branch of another principle – and on this there is disagreement.

Sixth: That the original case not fall outside the domain of analogical reasoning, such as devotional acts involving the number of prayer units, the prescribed amounts in legal punishments, and the like, as well as rulings specific to the Prophet – may Allah bless him and grant him peace.

Seventh: That the unifying attribute be present in the branch case just as it is in the original case.

Eighth: That the branch not be textually stipulated, for analogy is not considered in the presence of a textual proof (*naṣṣ*).

الفصل الثالث: في أنواعه

ونوضّحها بثلاث تقسيمات:

We clarify it through three divisions:

[FIRST DIVISION]

القسم الأوّل: ينقسم القياس إلى نوعين قياس علّة، وقياس شبه.

The First Division: Analogy (*qiyās*) is divided into two types: analogy by cause and analogy of resemblance.

فقيــاس العلّــة: هو الذي يكــون الجامع فيه بين الأصــل والفرع وصفًا هو علّة الحكم وموجب له كتحريم النبيذ المسكر بالقياس على الخمر، والجامع بينهما الإسكار وهو علّة التحريم.

Analogy by cause (*qiyās ʿillah*) is that in which the common element between the original case and the branch is a quality that constitutes the cause of the ruling and necessitates it – such as the prohibition of intoxicating date-wine by analogy to wine, the common element between them being intoxication, which is the cause of the prohibition.

وقياس الشبه: هو الذي يكون الجامع فيه وصفًا ليس بعلّة في الحكم كإيجــاب النيّة في الوضــوء بالقياس على التيمّم والجامــع بينهما أنّ كلّ واحد منهما طهارة من حدث، والطهارة من حدث ليســت علّةً لوجوب النيّة وإنّما هي وصف يشترك فيه الأصل والفرع.

Analogy of resemblance (*qiyās shabah*) is that in which the common element is an attribute that is not the cause of the ruling – such as the obligation of intention in ablution by analogy with dry ablution (*tayammum*), the commonality between them being that each is a purification from a state of ritual impurity (*ḥadath*). However, purification from ḥadath is not the cause for the obligation of intention; rather, it is an attribute shared by both the principal and the derivative.

واتّفق القائلون بالقياس على أنّ قياس العلّة حجّة، واختلفوا في الاحتجاج بقياس الشبه لضعفه، ولأنّه ينقلب، يقول الحنفيّ: لا تجب النيّة في الوضوء بالقياس على إزالة النجاسة، والجامع بينهما أنّ كلّ واحد منهما طهارة بالماء، وزاد بعض الأصوليّين نوعًا ثالثًا سمّوه قياس الدلالة، قال أبو المعالي: «لا معنى لِعَدِّه قسمًا على حدته، لأنّه تارةً يلحق بقياس العلّة وتارةً بقياس الشبه»، وزاد بعضهم قياس المناسبة وهو المبني على تحصيل مصلحة أو دفع مفسدة، وسنتكلّم عليه في المصلحة.

Those who affirm analogy agree that analogy by cause is a probative proof, but they differ regarding the probativity of analogy by resemblance due to its weakness and because it is reversible. For example, the Ḥanafī says that intention is not obligatory in ablution by analogy with the removal of impurity, the commonality between them being that each is a purification by water.

Some of the scholars of legal theory added a third type, which they called *analogy by indication* (*qiyās dalālah*). Abū al-Ma'ālī said: "There is no point in counting it as a separate category, because at times it is subsumed under analogy by cause and at times under analogy by resemblance."

Some also added *analogy by suitability* (*qiyās munāsabah*), which is based on the attainment of welfare (*maṣlaḥah*) or the repulsion of public detriment (*mafsadah*). We shall discuss it under the topic of public interest.[65]

---

65   See §4.10.

[SECOND DIVISION]

القسم الثاني: ينقسم من وجه آخر إلى نوعين: قياس جلي وقياس خفي، وهو بالنظر إلى ذلك على درجات.

The Second Division: It is divided from another aspect into two types: manifest analogy (*qiyās jalī*) and hidden analogy (*qiyās khafī*). In view of that, it is of varying degrees.

الدرجـة الأولـى: إثبات حكم المنطوق به للمسـكوت عنـه لأنّـه أولى كتحريم الضرب من قوله تعالى: ﴿فَلَا تَقُلْ لَهُمَا أُفٍّ﴾ [الإسراء ٢٣].

The first degree: Affirming the ruling of the stated case for the unstated case because it is more fitting – such as the prohibition of striking derived from His saying, exalted is He: "So do not say to them *'uff*."[66]

الدرجـة الثانيـة: إثبات حكم المنطوق به للمسـكوت عنه، لأنّه مثله كقول النبيّ -صلّى اللّه عليه وسـلّم-: «لا يبولنّ أحدكم في الماء الدائم ثـمّ يغسـل منه» فيحكم للمتغوط في المـاء الدائم بحكم البول لأنّه مثله في تنجيس الماء.

The second degree: Affirming the ruling of the stated case for the unstated case, because it is like it – such as the saying of the Prophet – may Allah bless him and grant him peace: "None of you should urinate in stagnant water and then wash from it." Thus, the same ruling is applied to one who defecates in stagnant water as to one who urinates in it, because it is like it in rendering the water impure.

وقد اختلف: هل تُسـمّى الدرجتان قياس أم لا تُسـمّى لظهورها حتى أنّ إلحاق المسكوت عنه بالمنطوق به فيها معلوم قطعًا لا يحتاج إلى فكر ولا استنباط علّة، ولا يخالف فيهما إلّا معاندًا أو جاهلًا.

---

66   Qurʾān, 17:23.

There is a disagreement: Are the two degrees called analogy or not, due to their clarity – such that the inclusion of the unspoken case under the spoken one in them is known with certainty, requiring neither reflection nor the derivation of a cause, and none disagrees concerning them except one who is obstinate or ignorant.

الدرجـة الثالثـة: قياس العلّة: وهو متفاوت في الخفاء والجلاء ألا ترى أنّ قيـاس الأرز علـى القمـح في تحريم التفاضل لعلّة الاقتيات والادّخار عنـد مالـك والطعميّة عند الشـافعيّ ليس في الظهـور كقياس النبيذ على الخمر لعلّة الإسكار.

The third degree: Analogy of cause (*qiyās 'illah*) varies in obscurity and clarity. Do you not see that the analogy of rice to wheat in the prohibition of excess exchange – due to the cause of edibility and storability according to Mālik, and gustatory quality according to al-Shāfi'ī – is not as manifest as the analogy of date wine (*nabīdh*) to grape wine (*khamar*) due to the cause of intoxication?

الدرجة الرابعة: قياس المناسبة، وهو أيضًا متفاوت.

The fourth degree: Analogy of suitability (*qiyās munāsabah*) also admits of gradation.

الدرجة الخامسة: قياس الشبه، وهو أيضًا متفاوت.

The fifth degree: Analogy of resemblance (*qiyās shabah*) also admits of gradation.

[THIRD DIVISION]

التقسيم الثالث: تعرف العلّة في قياس العلّة بأمور بعضها أقوى من بعض، متفاوت درجات القياس لذلك:

The Third Division: The cause is known in analogy of cause (*qiyās 'illah*) by several means, some of which are stronger than others. The degrees of analogy therefore vary:

الأوّل: النصّ على العلّة، كقول النبيّ -صلّى اللَّه عليه وسـلّم-: «إِنَّمَا جُعِلَ الإِذْنُ مِنْ أَجْلِ الْبَصَرِ».

First: Explicit mention of the cause, as in the saying of the Prophet – may Allah bless him and grant him peace: "Permission was instituted on account of sight."[67]

الثاني: الإيمـاء بالفـاء كقولـه تعالـى: ﴿وَالسَّارِقُ وَالسَّارِقَةُ فَاقْطَعُوا أَيْدِيَهُمَا﴾ [المائدة ٣٨]، أو بالباء كقوله: ﴿بِأَنَّهُمْ شَاقُّوا اللَّهَ وَرَسُـولَهُ﴾ [الأنفال ١٣]، أو باللام كقوله: ﴿وَمَا خَلَقْتُ الْجِنَّ وَالْإِنْسَ إِلَّا لِيَعْبُدُونِ﴾ [الذاريات ٥٦]، و«إنَّ» كقوله تعالى: ﴿إِنَّهُ كَانَ لَا يُؤْمِنُ بِاللَّهِ الْعَظِيمِ﴾ [الحاقة ٣٣].

Second: Indication by means of particles, such as:
- the *fā'*, as in His saying, exalted is He: "And the male thief and the female thief – so cut off their hands,"[68]
- the *bā'*, as in His saying: "Because they opposed Allah and His Messenger,"[69]
- the *lām*, as in His saying: "And I did not create the jinn and man-kind except that they should worship Me,"[70] and
- *inna*, as in His saying, exalted is He: "Indeed, he did not believe in Allah, the Tremendous."[71]

الثالـث: ترتيب الحكم على الوصـف كقوله عليه السلام: «الْقَاتِلُ لَا يَرِثُ» معناه لأجل قتله.

---

67 "Permission was instituted by Allah on account of sight." From Sahl ibn Saʿd: Muslim, 2156.

  "Seeking permission was instituted on account of sight." From Sahl ibn Saʿd: Aḥmad, 22854; al-Bukhārī, 5887; Muslim, 2156; al-Tirmidhī, 2709 – he said: *ḥasan ṣaḥīḥ*.

68 Qur'ān, 5:38.

69 Qur'ān, 8:13.

70 Qur'ān, 51:56.

71 Qur'ān, 69:33.

Third: The ordering of the ruling upon the attribute – as in his saying, may Allah bless him and grant him peace: "The killer does not inherit,"[72] meaning on account of his killing.

الرابع: الإجماع على العلّة.

Fourth: Consensus (*ijmāʿ*) on the cause (*ʿillah*).

الخامس: دوران الحكـم مع الوصف، وهو وجوده مع وجوده، وعدمه مع عدمه كالرجم مع الإحصان.

Fifth: The concomitance of the ruling with the attribute, namely, its existence with its existence and its nonexistence with its nonexistence – such as stoning with *iḥṣān*.[73]

السـادس: السـبر والتقسيم، وهو أن يقال: لا يخلو أن تكون علّة كذا وكذا، ويبطل أن تكون كذا، فيتعيّن أن يكون.

Sixth: *Elimination and division (sabr wa-taqsīm)*, which is to say: the cause of such-and-such must be one of a limited set of possibilities; then, one invalidates each possibility except one, whereby it is determined that it must be that one.

السابع: تقسيم المناط: وهو تعيين العلّة من بين أوصاف مذكورة كما ورد فـي الحديـث «أنّ أعرابيًّا جاء يضربُ صدرَه، وينتف شـعره، ويقول: هَلَكْـتُ وأُهْلَكْـتُ واقعـت أهلـي في رمضان» فهذه جملـة أوصاف تعيّن أنّ أمـره بالكفّـارة إنّمـا كان للجمـاع في رمضان لا لغيـره من الأوصاف المذكورة.

---

72   From Abū Hurayrah: al-Tirmidhī, 2109 – he said: not sound, only known through this chain; Ibn Mājah, 2645; al-Bayhaqī, 12023; al-Dāraquṭnī; al-Daylamī, 4692.

73   (Tr:) See your respective *madhhab*'s definition of *iḥṣān*.

Seventh: *Classification of the operative cause (taqsīm al-manāṭ):* This is the determination of the causal factor from among mentioned attributes, as in the ḥadīth: "A Bedouin came striking his chest, pulling out his hair, and saying, 'I am ruined and have ruined [others]; I had intercourse with my wife during Ramaḍān.'"[74] This is a set of attributes that determines that his being commanded to offer expiation was due to intercourse during Ramaḍān, and not due to any of the other mentioned attributes.

SUPPLEMENT

تكميل

يقول الفقهاء: تنقيح المناط وتخريج المناط وتحقيق المناط.

The jurists speak of refinement of the operative cause, derivation of the operative cause, and verification of the operative cause.

فأمّا تنقيح المناط فقد بيّناه، والمناط هو العلّة.

As for *refinement of the operative cause (tanqīḥ al-manāṭ)*, we have already explained it, and the operative cause (*manāṭ*) is the cause (*ʿillah*).

وأمّا تخريج المناط فهو تعيين العلّة من أوصاف غير مذكورة، كقوله ‑صلّى الله عليه وسلّم‑: «لا تَبِيعوا البُرَّ بالبُرِّ إلّا مِثْلًا بِمِثْلٍ»، فتنظر هل العلّة فى ذلك الطعميّة أو الاقتيات أو الكيل أو الوزن أو غير ذلك.

Derivation of the operative cause (takhrīj al-manāṭ) is the determination of the cause from among attributes not explicitly mentioned, such as in his (may Allah bless him and grant him peace) saying: "Do not sell wheat for wheat except like for like."[75] One then examines whether the cause in that is gustatory quality, nutritive value, measurability by volume, measurability by weight, or something else.

---

74   Ibn Abī Shaybah, 36182.
75   al-Bazzār, 3633.

وأمّا تحقيق المناط، فهو أن يتّفق على تعيين العلّة، ويطلب أن يثبت في محلّ النزاع.

Verification of the operative cause (taḥqīq al-manāṭ) is that there be agreement on the designation of the cause, and that it be sought to establish it in the point of contention.

4.7.4 ON THE INVALIDATORS OF ANALOGY

الفصل الرابع: في مفسدات القياس

وهي عشرة وبها ينقض الخصم قياس خصمه عند المناظرة:

They [the invalidators of analogy] are ten; by them the disputant refutes the analogies of his opponent during debate:

الأوّل: مخالف القياس لنصّ كتاب أو سنّة، فإن خالف قدّم الكتاب أو السـنّة لم يقدح ذلك فيه، لأنّ العموم يخصّص بالقياس على خلاف في ذلك، وقيل يخصّص وقيل يخصّص بالجلي لا بالخفي.

First: When analogy contradicts the text of the Book or the Sunnah: If it contradicts, yet the Book or Sunnah is given precedence, that does not invalidate the analogy, because a general statement is specified by analogy – though there is disagreement on this. It is said: it is specified; and it is said: it is specified by the manifest (*jalī*), not by the hidden (*khafī*).

والثاني: مخالف الإجماع.

Second: Its contradicts consensus.

والثالث: عدم ثبوت الوصف الجامع.

Third: The non-establishment of the unifying attribute.

والرابع: قصور العلّة، وهو كونها لا تتعدّى الأصل إلى سواه.

Fourth: The *deficiency of the cause (quṣūr al-ʿillah)*, which is its not extending beyond the principal case to anything else.

والخامس: النقض، وهو وجود الوصف بدون الحكم والنقض في سائر الأدلّة وجـود الدليل دون المدلـول، والنقض في الحدود وجود الحدّ دون المحدود وهو مفسد في الحدود، واختلف في إفساده في الأدلّة والعلل.

Fifth: *Refutation (naqḍ)* is the presence of the attribute without the ruling.

Refutation in other proofs is the presence of the proof without the thing proved; and refutation in definitions is the presence of the definition without the defined.

It is invalidating in definitions, and there is disagreement regarding its invalidation in proofs and causes.

والسادس: العكس: وهو وجود الحكم بدون الوصف، وإنّما يقدح إذا اتّفـق الخصمـان علـى أنّ العلّة واحدة فإذا وجد الحكم دونها دلّ على عـدم اعتبارهـا، وأمّـا إذا اتّفقا علـى أن لذلك الحكم علّتيـن أو أكثر فلا يقدح لاحتمال أن إحداهما خلفت الأخرى كالحيض يخلف الجنابة في وجوب الغسل لأنّهما علّتان في وجوب الغسل.

Sixth: The *inverse (ʿaks)* is the presence of the ruling without the attribute.

It is only a valid objection if both disputants agree that the cause is one; for if the ruling is found without it, this indicates that it is not to be considered. However, if they agree that the ruling has two or more causes, then it is not a valid objection, due to the possibility that one of them has replaced the other – such as menstruation replacing major ritual impurity in necessitating the ritual bath, since both are causes for the obligation of the ritual bath.

السـابع: القلـب: وهو إثبات نقيض الحكم بالعلّة بعينها، فإنّ ثبوت نقيضه معها يدلّ على استحالة ثبوته لأنّ النقيضين لا يجتمعان، وذلك

مثـل قـول المالكـيّ: الاعتكاف لبـث فـي مكان مخصوص فلا يسـتقلّ بنفسـه بالقيـاس علـى الوقـوف بعرفـة فيكـون الصائم شـرطًا فيـه فيقول: خصمـه: الاعتـكاف لبـث في مكان مخصـوص فلا يشـترط فيه الصوم بالقياس على الوقوف بعرفة.

Seventh: *Reversal* (*qalb*) is the affirmation of the contradictory (*naqīḍ*) of a ruling by means of the very same cause. For the affirmation of its contradictory along with it indicates the impossibility of its affirmation, since two contradictories cannot coexist.

An example of this is the statement of the Mālikī: "Retreat (*i'tikāf*) is a remaining in a specific place, so it is not independent in itself, by analogy with standing at 'Arafah; thus, fasting is a condition for it." His opponent replies: "Retreat (*i'tikāf*) is a remaining in a specific place, so fasting is not a condition for it, by analogy with standing at 'Arafah."

الثامـن: الفـرق: وهـو إبداء معنى مناسـب للحكم يوجـد في الأصل ويعـدم فـي الفـرع، أو يوجد فـي الفرع ويعدم فـي الأصل كقول الحنفيّ: الوضوء طهارة بالماء فلا يفتقر إلى نيّة كإزالة النجاسة، فيجيبه الفارق بأنّ الوضوء طهارة حكميّة وإزالة النجاسـة طهارة عينيّة فافترق حكمهما، فإن كان الفرق غير مناسـب لم يقدح في القياس كقول القائل: الأرز مقتات فيحرم فيه التفاضل كالقمح، فيقول الفارق: الفرق بينهما أنّ الأرز شديد البياض بخلاف القمح، فهذا خلاف لا يعتبر.

Eighth: *Distinction* (*farq*) is the presentation of a meaning appropriate to the ruling, which is present in the principal case and absent in the derivative, or present in the derivative and absent in the principal.

An example is the Ḥanafī's statement: "*Wuḍū'* is purification with water, so it does not require intention, like the removal of filth." The one who distinguishes replies: "*Wuḍūʾ* is a legal (*ḥukmī*) purification, whereas the removal of filth is a concrete (*ʿaynī*) purification, so their rulings differ."

If the distinction is not appropriate, it does not invalidate the analogy, such as when one says: "Rice is a staple food, so unlawful gain (*ribā*) applies to it like wheat." The one who distinguishes replies: "The difference between them is that rice is intensely white, unlike wheat." This is a distinction that is not considered.

التاســع: القــول: بالموجب: وهو يقدح في جميــع الأدلّة من القياس وغيره، ومعناه أن يُسَـلَّمَ الخصم الدليل الذي استدلّ به المسـتدلّ إلّا أن يقــول هــذا الدليل ليس في محلّ النزاع، إنّما هو في غيره فيبقي الخلاف بينهما، كقول الشافعيّ: المحرّم إذا مات لم يغسل ولم يمس بطيب لقول رسول اللَّه -صلّى اللَّه عليه وسلّم- في رجل مات وهو محرّم: «لا تمسّوه بطيب، فإنّه يبعث يوم القيامة ملبيًّا»، فيقول المالكيّ: سلّمنا ذلك الرجل وإنّما النزاع في غيره، لأنّ اللفظ لم يرد بصيغة العموم.

Ninth: Concession by the entailment (*qawl bi-l-mūjib*): This undermines all proofs, whether analogical (*qiyās*) or otherwise. Its meaning is that the opponent concedes the proof presented by the proponent, except that he says: "This proof does not pertain to the point of contention; rather, it pertains to something else." Thus, the disagreement remains between them.

An example is in al-Shāfiʿī's statement: If the one in a state of pilgrimage consecration (*muḥrim*) dies, he is not to be washed and not to be touched with perfume, due to the saying of the Messenger of Allah (may Allah bless him and grant him peace) concerning a man who died while in a state of consecration: "Do not apply perfume to him, for he will be resurrected on the Day of Resurrection proclaiming the *talbiyah*."[76]

---

76   From Ibn ʿAbbās: al-Nasāʾī, 1904.

The Mālikī says: "We concede the case of that man; however, the dispute concerns others, because the wording was not expressed in a form indicating generality."

العاشر: نقص شرط من شروط القياس، وقد عدّدناها في مواضعها.

Tenth: The absence of a condition from among the conditions of analogy, which we have enumerated in their respective places.[77]

4.8 ON INFERENCE   الباب الثامن: في الاستدلال

وهو محاولة الدليل المفضي إلى الحكم، ويقال باصطلاحين:

أحدهمـا: محاولـة الدليل الشـرعيّ أو غيرها من جهـة القواعد لا من جهة الأدلّة المعلومة، وهو قصدنا هنا.

والثاني: محاولة الدليل الشرعيّ وغيره من الأدلّة المعلومة أو غيرها.

It [*inference (istidlāl)*] is the attempt at a proof that leads to a ruling, and it is expressed in two technical senses.

First: The attempt at the revealed proof or other than it from the perspective of principles (*qawāʿid*), not from the perspective of known evidences – and this is our intent here.

Second: The attempt at the Legal proof and other known proofs or otherwise.

والثاني أعمّ والأوّل أخصّ، وهو على ضربين:

The second is more general, and the first is more specific.

It is of two kinds:

[FIRST KIND]

الضرب الأوّل: الاستدلال بالملزوم على لازمه، وباللازم على ملزومه.

---

77   See §4.7.2.

The first kind: Inference from the concomitant antecedent (*malzūm*) to its concomitant consequent (*lāzim*), and from the concomitant consequent to its concomitant antecedent.

والملزوم ما يحسن معه «لو» واللازم ما يحسن معه «اللام» نحو: ﴿لَوْ كَانَ فِيهِمَا آلِهَةٌ إِلَّا اللَّهُ لَفَسَدَتَا﴾ [الأنبياء ٢٢]، وكقولنا: «إن كان هذا الطعام مهلكًا فهو حرام»، تقديره: «لو كان مهلكًا لكان حرامًا»، ويتصوّر في ذلك أربع صور: اثنان منتجان وهما: الاستدلال بوجود الملزوم على وجود اللازم، وبعدم اللازم على عدم الملزوم، واثنان عقيمان لا ينتجان وهما: الاستدلال بعدم الملزوم أو بوجود اللازم إلّا أن يكون اللازم مساويًا للملزوم ينتج الأربعة نحو: لو كان هذا إنسانًا لكان ضاحكًا.

The *concomitant antecedent* (*malzūm*) is that with which "if" (*law*) is appropriate.

The *concomitant consequent* (*lāzim*) is that with which "then" (*lām*) is appropriate.

It is as in: "If there were in them any gods other than Allah, they would surely have been corrupted,"[78] and as in our saying: "If this food is lethal, then it is forbidden" – its estimation being: "If it were lethal, it would be forbidden."

There are four conceivable configurations in this regard, two of which are productive: reasoning from the existence of the concomitant antecedent to the existence of the concomitant consequent, and reasoning from the nonexistence of the concomitant consequent to the nonexistence of the concomitant antecedent. Two are barren and yield nothing: inference from the nonexistence of the concomitant antecedent, and inference from the existence of the concomitant consequent – unless the concomitant consequent is equivalent to the concomitant antecedent, in which case all four forms yield, such as: "If this were a human, it would be laughing."

---

78   Qurʾān, 21:22.

ثمّ إنّ الملازمة قد تكون قطعيّةً وظنّيّةً، والموجود هنا ما كان منفيًّا في اللفـظ والمعـدوم مـا كان ثابتًا في اللفظ، لأنّ «لـو» تنفي الثابت وتثبت المنفيّ.

Furthermore, concomitance may be certain (*qaṭʿī*) or presumptive (*ẓannī*).

What is present here is that which is negated in expression, and what is nonexistent is that which is affirmed in expression – because "if" (*law*) negates the affirmed and affirms the negated.

[SECOND KIND]

الضرب الثاني: السـبر والتقسـيم: وهو حصر الأقسام بين النفي والإثبات حتى يحصل المطلوب، كقولنا: «لا يخلو أن يكون كذا وكذا»، و «باطل أن يكـون كـذا وكـذا» يثبـت ضدّه وهو كـذا، أو يبطل جميع الأقسـام، وكلّ واحد من الضربين حجّة صحيحة وهما الشـرط المتّصل والمنفصل المذكوران في العقليّات.

The second kind: *Elimination and division (sabr wa-taqsīm)* is the restriction of the possible divisions between negation and affirmation until the intended conclusion is obtained, as in our saying: "It must be either such-and-such or such-and-such," and "It is invalid for it to be such-and-such." Its opposite is then established, namely, "such-and-such"; or all the divisions are invalidated.

Each of the two types is a valid proof – namely, the conjoining conditional (*sharṭ muttaṣil*) and the disjoining conditional (*sharṭ munfaṣil*) mentioned in the speculative rational sciences.

4.9   ON PRESUMPTION OF CONTINUITY, PRESUMPTIVE NON-LIABILITY, PREFERENCE FOR THE LIGHTER OPTION, INDUCTION, AND JURISTIC PREFERENCE

الباب التاسع: في الاستصحاب، والبراءة الأصليّة، والأخذ بالأخفّ، والاستقراء، والاستحسان

ON PRESUMPTION OF CONTINUITY

أمّا الاسـتصحاب: فهو بقاء الأمر والحال والاسـتقبال على ما كان عليه فـي الماضـي وهـو قولهم: «الأصل بقاء ما كان علـى ما كان حتى يدلّ الدليل على خلاف ذلك» وهو حجّة عند المالكيّة وأكثر الشافعيّة خلافًا للحنفيّة والمتكلّمين.

Presumption of continuity (istiṣḥāb) is the persistence of a matter, a state, or a future condition upon what it was in the past.

It is their saying: "The presumption is the persistence of what was upon what it was, until evidence indicates otherwise."

It is a probative proof according to the Mālikīs and most of the Shāfiʿīs, in opposition to the Ḥanafīs and the theologians (*mutakallimūn*).

ON PRESUMPTIVE NON-LIABILITY

وأمّا البراءة الأصليّة، فهي ضرب من الاستصحاب، ومعناها: البقاء على عـدم الحكـم حتـى يدلّ الدليل عليـه، لأنّ الأصل بـراءة الذمّة من لزوم الأحكام، وهي حجّة خلافًا للمعتزلة وأبي الفرج والأُبَهَريّ المالكيّين.

Presumptive non-liability (barāʾah aṣliyyah) is a type of presumption of continuity (*istiṣḥāb*). Its meaning is the persistence of the absence of a ruling until evidence indicates it, because the default is the immunity of liability from the obligation of rulings.

It is a valid probative proof, contrary to the view of the Muʿtazilah, Abū al-Faraj, and al-Abharī of the Mālikī school.

ON PREFERENCE FOR THE LIGHTER OPTION

وأمّـا الأخـذ بالأخفّ، فهـو ضـرب من البـراءة الأصليّة، ومعنـاه: الأخذ بأخفّ الأقـوال حتى يـدلّ الدليل على الانتقال إلـى الأثقل، وهو حجّة عند الشافعيّة.

Preference for the lighter option (al-akhaf bi-l-akhaf) is a kind of presumptive non-liability.

Its meaning is to adopt the lighter of the opinions until evidence indicates the transition to the heavier.

It is considered a probative proof by the Shāfiʿīs.

ON INDUCTION

وأمّـا الاسـتقراء: فهـو تتبّـع الحكم فـي مواضعه، فيوجد فيهـا على حالة واحـدة حتـى يغلـب على الظـنّ أنّه محلّ النزاع على تلـك الحالة، وهي حجّة عند الشافعيّة.

Induction (istiqrāʾ) is the tracing of a ruling across its instances, wherein it is found in a single state, such that it predominates in the mind that the point of contention is likewise in that state.[79]

It is considered a probative proof by the Shāfiʿīs.

ON JURISTIC PREFERENCE

وأمّـا الاستحسـان، فهـو حجّـة عند أبـي حنيفـة خلافًا لغيـره حتى قال الشـافعيّ: «من استحسـن فقد شـرّع» ثمّ اختلف الناس في معناه، فقال الباجـي: «هـو القـول بأقوى الدليليـن» وعلـى هذا يكون حجّـة إجماعًا. وقيـل: هـو الحكم بغير دليل، وعلـى هذا يكون حرامًا إجماعًا، لأنّه اتّباع

---

79 See §1.8.

للهوى، وقيل: هو دليل ينقدح في نفس المجتهد لا تساعده العبارة عنه.
وأشبه الأقوال إنّه ما يستحسنه المجتهد بعقله.

Juristic preference (istiḥsān) is a probative proof according to Abū Ḥanīfah, contrary to others – to the extent that al-Shāfiʿī said: "Whoever employs juristic preference (*istiḥsān*) has legislated."[80] Thereafter people differed regarding its meaning.

Al-Bājī[81] said: "It is the assertion of the stronger of two proofs." According to this, it would be a proof by consensus.

It was also said: It is judgement without any proof. According to this, it would be prohibited by consensus, because it is following caprice.

And it was said: It is a proof (*dalīl*) that arises in the mind of the independent jurist but which he cannot articulate.

The view most resembling the truth is that it is what the independent jurist deems preferable by his intellect (*ʿaql*).

---

80   (Tr:) In his *Mukhtaṣar*, al-Muzanī (d. 264/878) writes: "It is not permissible for him to exercise juristic preference (*istiḥsān*) without analogical reasoning (*qiyās*), for were that permissible, it would amount to legislating in the religion." The editor notes that this is likely the source from which later authorities abridged al-Shāfiʿī's famous dictum: "Whoever exercises juristic preference has legislated" (*man istaḥsana fa-qad sharraʿa*). Imām al-Ḥaramayn confirms this in *al-Nihāyah*, adding that the core of *istiḥsān* amounts to considerations of public welfare (*istiṣlāḥ*) with no basis in the Law, and that subordinating sound *qiyās* to such considerations is what al-Shāfiʿī condemned. See Abū Ibrāhīm Ismāʿīl ibn Yaḥyā al-Muzanī, *Al-Mukhtaṣar min ʿilm al-Shāfiʿī wa-min maʿnā qawlihi*, ed. Abū ʿĀmir ʿAbdallāh Sharaf al-Dīn al-Dāghistānī (Riyadh: Dār Madārij, 1440/2019), 2:628.

81   Abū al-Walīd Sulaymān ibn Khalaf al-Bājī, *Al-Ishārah fī maʿrifat al-uṣūl wa-al-wajāzah fī maʿnā al-dalīl*, ed. Muḥammad ʿAlī Farkūs (Mecca: al-Maktabah al-Makkiyyah; Beirut: Dār al-Bashāʾir al-Islāmiyyah, 1416/1996), 312.

<table>
<tr><td>

4.10   ON CUSTOMS,
UNRESTRICTED PUBLIC
INTEREST, BLOCKING
THE MEANS, AND
INFALLIBILITY

</td><td>

الباب العاشر: في العوائد
والمصلحة المرسلة، وسدّ الذرائع،
والعصمة

</td></tr>
</table>

ON CUSTOMS

أمّـا العوائـد: فهـي غلبة معنى مـن المعاني على النـاس، وقد تكون هذه
الغلبـة فـي جميـع الأقاليـم، وقد تختصّ ببعض البلاد أو بعـض الفرق،
فيقضي بالعادة عند المالكيّة خلافًا لغيرهم، وذلك ما لم تخالف الشريعة.

Customs (*'awā'id*) are the predominance of a particular practices
among people. This predominance may occur across all regions, or
it may be specific to certain lands or particular sects.

The Mālikīs rule according to custom, contrary to others, provided
it does not contravene the Sharīʿah.

ON PUBLIC INTEREST

وأمّا المصلحة، فهي على ثلاثة أقسام:

Public interest (*maṣlaḥah*) is of three kinds.

[ATTESTED INTERESTS]

(١) قسـم شـهد الشـرع باعتباره، وهو قياس المناسـبة المبني على النظر
المصلحيّ من تحصيل المصالح ودفع المفاسد، فهذا حجّة عند جميع
القائليـن بالقيـاس، ومـن ذلـك ما فعله عمر رضـي اللَّه عنه مـن الديوان
وإحداث السجن وغير ذلك.

(1) A category attested by the Law for its consideration is the
analogy of suitability (*qiyās munāsabah*), which is based on speculative reasoning concerning public interest (*maṣlaḥah*) – namely, the
attainment of public interests and the repulsion of public detriments.

This is a probative proof according to all who affirm analogy.

Among its instances is what ʿUmar – may Allah be pleased with him – enacted of the register (*dīwān*),[82] the institution of imprisonment, and other such matters.

[VOIDED INTERESTS]

(٢) وقسم شهد الشرع بعدم اعتباره كالمنع من غراسة العنب لئلّا يعصر منه خمرًا، فهذا لا يقول به.

(2) A category which the Law has testified to be of no consideration, such as the prohibition of planting grapevines lest wine be pressed from them – this is not affirmed.

[UNATTESTED INTERESTS]

(٣) وقسم لـم يشـهد الشـرع باعتبـاره ولا بعدم اعتباره، وهـو المصلحة المرسـلة، وهـو حجّة عند مالك خلافًا لغيـره وقال أبو حامد: «إن وقعت فـي محـلّ الحاجة والتتمّة لم يعتبر، كان وقعت في محلّ الضرورة فيجوز أن يؤدّي إليها اجتهاد مجتهد، والضرورة هي الخمسة التي اتّفقت عليها الشـرائع، وهـي حفـظ الأديـان والنفوس والأنسـاب والأمـوال والعقول»، واشترط أبو حامد في المصلحة أن تكون كلّيّةً قطعيّةً مع كونها ضروريّةً.

(3) A category not attested by the Law as either valid or invalid is the *unattested public interest* (*maṣlaḥah mursalah*).

It is considered probative proof by Mālik, contrary to others.

Abū Ḥāmid said: "If it occurs in a context of need or supplementation, it is not to be considered; but if it occurs in a context of necessity, then it is possible that the *ijtihād* of an independent jurist may lead to it. Necessity refers to the five matters upon which the revealed laws have agreed: the preservation of religion, the preservation of

---

82   (Tr:) The *dīwān* is the register of warriors and their stipends that ʿUmar ibn al-Khaṭṭāb instituted to organise the distribution of state revenue.

life, the preservation of lineage, the preservation of wealth, and the preservation of intellect."

Abū Ḥāmid stipulated that the public interest must be: universal, definitive, and necessary.

ON BLOCKING THE MEANS

وأمّا سدّ الذرائع بمعناه: حسم مادّة الفساد بقطع وسائله.

Blocking the means (*sadd al-dharā'i'*), in its meaning, it is the elimination of the source of corruption by cutting off its means.

والذرائع هي الوسائل، وهي على ثلاثة أقسام:

١. أحدها معتبر إجماعًا كسبّ الأصنام عند من يعلم من حاله أنّه يسبّ اللّه.

٢. وقسم غير معتبر إجماعًا كالمنع من الشركة في سكنى الديار مخافة الزنى.

٣. وقسم مختلف فيه كبيوع الآجال فاعتبرها مالك خلافًا لغيره.

The *means* (*dharā'i'*) are instruments, and they are of three categories:

1. One deemed valid by consensus, such as reviling idols in the presence of one who is known to revile Allah in return.
2. A category unanimously deemed not of consideration, such as the prohibition of cohabitation in dwellings out of fear of fornication.
3. A category subject to disagreement, such as deferred-payment sales, which Mālik deemed valid, contrary to others.

NOTE تنبيه

ينقل أهل المذهب عن مالك أنّه انفرد باعتبار العوائد والمصلحة والذريعة وليس كذلك، فإنّ العادة هي العرف، وهو معتبر في المذاهب، والمصلحة

قد اعتبرها أهل المذاهب قسمًا منها، وإنّما انفرد مالك بقسم، فحاصل هذا أنّه اعتبر المصلحة والذريعة أكثر من غيره لا أنّه انفرد بهما.

The adherents of the school report from Mālik that he uniquely considered custom, public interest, and pretext. But this is not the case.

For *custom* (*ʿādah*) is *convention* (*ʿurf*), and it is taken into account in the schools.

As for public interest (*maṣlaḥah*), the adherents of the schools have considered it a category thereof. Mālik merely singled out a particular category. The upshot is that he considered benefit and pretext more than others, not that he was unique in considering them.

ON INFALLIBILITY

وأمّا العصمة، فمعناها أن يقول اللَّه لنبيّ أو لعالم: «احكم فإنّك لا تحكم إلّا بالصواب لأنّي عصمتك من الخطأ».

وقد اختلف الناس في ذلك، فقال بوقوع ذلك مويس بن عمران والروافض، وقالت المعتزلة: وذلك ممتنع، وتوقّف الشافعيّ ووافقه فخر الدين بن الخطيب.

Infallibility (*ʿiṣmah*): its meaning is that Allah says to a prophet or to a scholar: "Judge, for you do not judge except with correctness, for I have protected you from error."

People have differed on that matter. Muways ibn ʿImrān and the Rāfiḍites affirmed its occurrence, while the Muʿtazilites said it is impossible. Al-Shāfiʿī withheld judgement, and Fakhr al-Dīn ibn al-Khaṭīb agreed with him.

5

ON INDEPENDENT REASONING,

FOLLOWING AUTHORITY, LEGAL RESPONSES,

CONFLICT, AND PREFERENTIAL WEIGHING

الفنّ الخامس من علم الأصول في الاجتهاد،
والتقليد، والفتوى، والتعارض والترجيح

وفيه عشرة أبواب:

It comprises ten sections.

5.1   ON INDEPENDENT JURISTIC REASONING

الباب الأوّل: في الاجتهاد

وهـو اسـتفراغ الوسـع في النظـر في الأحكام الشـرعيّة، وهـو واجب عند
مالك، وجمهور العلماء على تفصيل نذكره بعد هذا.

Ijtihād (independent juristic reasoning) is the exertion of utmost effort in the examination of legal rulings. It is obligatory according to Mālik and the majority of the scholars, with details which we shall mention subsequently.

 فروع

الأوّل: لا خلاف في جواز الاجتهاد بعد وفاة رسول اللَّه -صلّى اللَّه عليه وسلّم- وأمّا اجتهاد غيره في زمانه، فان كان غائبًا عنه جـاز، وإن كان حاضرًا معه ففيه خلاف.

First: There is no disagreement regarding the permissibility of *ijtihād* after the death of the Messenger of Allah – may Allah bless him and grant him peace.

As for the *ijtihād* of someone other than him during his lifetime, if that person was absent from him, it was permissible; but if he was present with him, then there is disagreement concerning it.

الفرع الثاني: قال الشافعيّ وأبو يوسف وغيرهما: يجوز أن يحكم النبيّ -صلّى اللَّه عليه وسلّم- بالاجتهاد، وقال آخرون لـم يكن متعبّدًا به لأنّ الوحي يغني عن الاجتهاد.

Second Branch: Al-Shāfiʿī, Abū Yūsuf, and others said: It is permissible for the Prophet (may Allah bless him and grant him peace) to judge by means of *ijtihād*. Others said: he was not religiously obligated to do so, for revelation obviates the need for *ijtihād*.

الفـرع الثالـث: إذا نُقـل عـن المجتهد قـولان، فإن علـم التاريخ عُدَّ الثانـي رجوعًـا عـن الأوّل. وإن لـم يعلم حكـي عنه القـولان ولم يحكم عليـه برجـوع، وإن كان في وقت واحد بمعنى أنّ المسألة عنده محتملة للقولين، وإن أشار إلى ترجيح أحدهما نقل عنه، وإلّا نقل عنه القولان.

Third Branch: If two opinions are transmitted from the independent jurist; the individual exercising *ijtihād*, then if the chronology is known, the second is deemed a retraction of the first. If the chronology is not known, both opinions are reported from him without judging it a retraction. And if they occurred at the same time – meaning that the issue, in his view, admits both opinions – and he indicated preference for one of them, that one is transmitted from him. Otherwise, both opinions are transmitted from him.

الفــرع الرابــع: إذا أفتى المجتهد في مسألة ثمّ ســئل عنها مرّةً أخرى، فإن كان ذاكرًا لاجتهاده الأوّل أفتى به، كان نســيه اســتأنف الاجتهاد، فإن أداه إلى خلاف الأوّل أفتي بالثاني.

Fourth Branch: If the independent jurist issues a *fatwā* on a matter and is then asked about it again, if he remembers his first *ijtihād*, he issues a *fatwā* accordingly. But if he has forgotten it, he recommences *ijtihād*. If this leads him to a conclusion contrary to the first, he issues a *fatwā* based on the second.

5.2	ON THE CONDITIONS OF THE INDEPENDENT JURIST	الباب الثاني: في شروط المجتهد

وهي على الجملة أربعة: التكليّف، والثاني العدالة، والثالث جودة الحفظ، والرابع المعرفة بما يتوقّف عليها الاجتهاد من العلوم، وهي خمسة فنون:

They are, in general, four: legal responsibility, uprightness, soundness of memory, and knowledge of the sciences upon which *ijtihād* depends, which are five disciplines.

[THE DEPENDENT SCIENCES OF IJTIHĀD]
[THE BOOK OF ALLAH]

أوّلهــا: كتــاب اللَّـه تعالــى فلا بدّ مــن حفظه، وتجويد قراءتـه ولو بحرف واحد من الأحرف الســبعة، وفهم معانيه لا ســيّما آيات الأحكام، ومعرفة المكيّ والمدنيّ منه، ومعرفة المحكم، والناسخ والمنسوخ منه وغير ذلك من علومه.

First Discipline: The Book of Allah, exalted is He. It is necessary to memorise it, to perfect its recitation – even if by a single mode from the seven modes – and to understand its meanings, especially the verses of rulings; and to know which parts are Meccan and which are Medinan; and to know the perspicuous [and the ambiguous], the abrogating and abrogated therein, and other such sciences related to it.

وقــال قـوم من الأصوليّين: لا يشــترط حفظه للقــرآن ولا حفظه لآيات الأحــكام منــه بل العلم بمواضعه لينظر فيها الحاجة إليها، وهذا خطأ من وجهين:

A group of the scholars of legal theory (*uṣūlīs*) said: It is not a condition that he have memorised the Qurʾān, nor that he have memorised the verses of rulings from it, but rather that he know their locations so that he may consult them when the need arises. This is erroneous from two perspectives:

أحدهما: أنّ الأحكام قد تخرج من غير الآيات المعلومة فيها فيضطرّ إلى حفظ الجميع.

First: That rulings may be derived from verses other than the well-known ones, necessitating the memorisation of all.

والآخــر: أنّ مَـن زهد في حفــظ كتاب اللَّه كما ينبغي أن يكون إمامًا في دين اللَّه، كيف وقد قال رسول اللَّه -صلّى اللَّه عليه وسلّم-: «كِتَابُ اللَّهِ هُوَ حَبْلُ اللَّهِ الْمَتِينُ، وَصِرَاطُهُ الْمُسْتَقِيمُ، فِيهِ خَبَرُ مَنْ قَبْلَكُمْ وَنَبَأُ مَنْ بَعْدَكُــمْ، وَحُكْــمُ مَــا بَيْنَكُمْ، مَنْ تَرَكَـهُ مِنْ جَبَّارٍ قَصَمَهُ اللَّـهُ، وَمَن ابْتَغَى الهُدَى مِنْ غَيْرِهِ أَضَلَّهُ اللَّهُ» حسـبك هذا الوعيد لمَن تركه وابتغى الهدى من غيره.

Second: That whoever is indifferent to preserving the Book of Allah as it ought to be preserved – how can such a one be an Imām in the religion of Allah? Especially when the Messenger of Allah (may Allah bless him and grant him peace) said:

The Book of Allah is the firm rope of Allah and His straight path.
In it is the account of those before you, the news of those after
you, and the ruling between you. Whoever abandons it out of
tyranny, Allah will crush him; and whoever seeks guidance
from other than it, Allah will lead him astray.[83]

This warning suffices for the one who abandons it and seeks
guidance from other than it.

[HADĪTHS RELATED TO LEGAL MATTERS]

وثانيها : حفـظ حديـث رسـول اللَّه -صلَّى اللَّـه عليه وسـلَّم-، وأحاديث
أصحابـه، وحفظ أسـانيدها، ومعرفة الرجال الناقليـن لهما، على أن أئمَّة
المحدّثين رضي اللَّه عنهم وجزاهم خيرًا، قد قاموا بوظيفة معرفة الناقلين،
وتجريحهـم وتعديلهـم، وتمييـز الحديث الصحيح من غيـره، وتدوينه في
تصانيفهم حين كفوا من بعدهم مؤنة معرفة الأسانيد والرجال، وصار ذلك
للمجتهد صفة كمال.

Second Discipline: Memorising the ḥadīth of the Messenger of
Allah (may Allah bless him and grant him peace) and the ḥadīths
of his Companions, memorising their chains of transmission, and
knowing the transmitters of both. The Imāms of ḥadīth – may Allah be
pleased with them and reward them well – have already undertaken
the task of identifying the transmitters, critiquing and accrediting
them, distinguishing sound ḥadīths from others, and recording them
in their compilations, thereby sparing those who came after them the
burden of verifying the chains of transmission and the transmitters.
This has thus become, for the independent jurist, a trait of perfection.

---

83   From ‘Alī: Ibn Abī Shaybah, 30007; al-Dārimī, 3331; al-Tirmidhī, 2906 – he
     said: *gharīb*, its *isnād* is *majhūl*, and there is criticism regarding al-Ḥārith;
     al-Bayhaqī, *Shu‘ab al-Īmān*, 1935.

وقال قوم: لا يشترط في المجتهد حفظ الحديث، وهذا أيضًا خطأ، فإن أكثر الأحكام منصوصة في الحديث، فإذا لم يعرف الحديث أفتى بالقياس أو غيره من الأدلّة الضعيفة وخالف النصّ النبويّ.

A group said: It is not a condition for the independent jurist to have memorised ḥadīth. This also is an error, for most rulings are explicitly stated in the ḥadīth. If he does not know the ḥadīth, he will issue legal opinions based on analogy (*qiyās*) or other weak evidences, thereby contravening the Prophetic text.

[JURISPRUDENCE]

وثالثها: المعرفة بالفقه، وحفظ مذاهب العلماء في الأحكام الشرعيّة ليقتدي في مذاهبه بالسلف الصالح، وليختار في أقوالهم ما هو أصحّ وأرجح، ولئلّا يخرج عن أقوالهم بالكلّيّة، فيخرق الإجماع، وقد كان مالك على جلالته يقتدي بمن تقدّمه من العلماء، ويتّبع مذاهبهم.

Third Discipline: Knowledge of jurisprudence (*fiqh*), and memorisation of the doctrines of the scholars regarding the legal rulings, so that he may follow in his doctrines the righteous predecessors, and choose among their statements that which is sounder and more preponderant, and so that he does not depart entirely from their statements, thereby violating consensus (*ijmāʿ*). Mālik, despite his eminence, used to follow those scholars who preceded him and adhere to their doctrines.

[THE PRINCIPLES OF JURISPRUDENCE]

ورابعها: المعرفة بأصول الفقه، فإنّه الآلة التي يتوصّل بها للاجتهاد.

Fourth Discipline: Knowledge of the principles of jurisprudence (*uṣūl al-fiqh*), for it is the instrument by which one attains *ijtihād*.

[ARABIC LANGUAGE]

وخامسها: المعرفة بما يحتاج إليه من علوم لسان العرب من النحو واللغة
ليفهم بذلك القرآن والحديث إذ هما بلسان العرب.

Fifth Discipline: Knowledge of what is required from the sciences of the Arabic tongue, such as the grammar and lexicon, in order to understand thereby the Qur'ān and ḥadīth, for both are in the language of the Arabs.

[OTHER SCIENCES]

وأمّا معرفته بغير ما ذكرنا من العلوم فليست شرطًا في الاجتهاد في
الأحكام الشرعيّة، ولكنّها صفة كمال، ومن أراد الاجتهاد في فنّ من
الفنون فلا بدّ له من معرفته ومعرفة رواته.

Knowledge of sciences other than what we have mentioned is not a condition for *ijtihād* in legal rulings, but rather a perfectional attribute. And whoever desires *ijtihād* in a particular discipline must necessarily know it and know its transmitters.

<table>
<tr><td>5.3</td><td>ON THE CORRECTNESS OF
THE INDEPENDENT JURISTS
IN LEGAL RULINGS</td><td dir="rtl">الباب الثالث: في تصويب
المجتهدين في الأحكام</td></tr>
</table>

الأحكام الشرعيّة ضربان: عقليّة وهي أصل الدين، وسمعيّة وهو فروع
الفقه.

Legal rulings are of two kinds:

1. *rational* (*ʿaqliyyah*), which constitute the foundation of religion (*uṣūl al-dīn*); and
2. *scriptural* (*samʿiyyah*), which pertain to the branches of jurisprudence (*furūʿ al-fiqh*).

فأمّــا أصــول الدين كإثبــات الصانع ووحدانيته وصفاتـه، وإثبات النبوّة وغير ذلك، فإنّ الحقّ فيها في قول واحد وما عدا ذلك باطل، وعلى ذلك اتّفق العلماء إلّا الجاحظ والعنبريّ فإنّهما قال: «كلّ مجتهد مصيب في أصول الدين»، بمعنى نفي الإثم لا بمعنى مطابقة الاعتقاد للحقّ.

As for the fundamentals of religion – such as the affirmation of the Maker, His oneness, His attributes, the affirmation of prophethood, and the like – the truth in these matters lies in a single position, and all else is false. The scholars have agreed upon this, with the exception of al-Jāḥiẓ and al-ʿAnbarī, for they said: "Every independent jurist is correct in the fundamentals of religion," meaning the negation of sin, not the correspondence of belief to the truth.

وأمّا الفروع فهي على ثلاثة أضرب:

As for the subsidiary matters, they are of three kinds.

(١) ضــرب لا يسوغ الاجتهــاد فيــه لأنّـه علم من الديـن بالضرورة، كوجـوب الصلـوات الخمس وصيام رمضان وتحريـم الخمر، فمَن خالف في شــيء من ذلك فهو مخطئ بإجماع ويكفر، لأنّ المخالفة في ذلك تكذيب للّه ولرسوله -صلّى اللّه عليه وسلّم-.

(1) A category in which independent reasoning is not permissible, because it is known from religion by necessity (ḍarūrah) – such as the obligation of the five daily prayers, the fasting of Ramaḍān, and the prohibition of wine. Whoever opposes any of that is in error by consensus and is deemed a disbeliever, because opposition in such matters constitutes a denial of Allah and His Messenger – may Allah bless him and grant him peace.

(٢) وضــرب لــم يعلــم مــن الدين ضــرورةً، ولكنّـه أجمـع عليه جميع الأمّة في جميع الأعصار والأمصار كوجوب الصداق في النكاح، وتحريم

المطلقــة ثلاثًـا إلّا بعــد زوج، وغير ذلك، فهذا ضرب مَن خالف فيه فهو
مخطئ بإجماع وهو فاسق.

(2) A category not known from religion by necessity (*ḍarūrah*), but upon which the entire community (*ummah*) has unanimously agreed across all eras and lands – such as the obligation of the dower (*ṣadāq*) in marriage, the prohibition of a thrice-divorced woman except after marriage to another husband, and the like. This is a category wherein one who dissents is in error by consensus and is a transgressor (*fāsiq*).

(٣) وضرب يسوغ فيه الاجتهاد وهي المسائل التي اختلف فيها فقهاء الأمصــار علــى قولين فأكثــر، ففي التصويــب في هذا الضــرب اختلاف العلماء، فقال قوم: «إنّ الحقّ في ذلك كلّه واحد وما عداه باطل، ولكن المخطئ فيه غير مأثوم» وهو مذهب الشــافعيّ، وقال قوم: «كلّ مجتهد مصيب»، وهو قول أبي حنيفة وأبي الحسـن الأشـعريّ والقاضي أبي بكر وأكثر المتكلّمين، ونقل عن مالك القولان.

(3) A category in which *ijtihād* is permissible: namely, the issues over which the jurists of the various regions have differed into two or more opinions. Regarding the correctness (*taṣwīb*) in this category, the scholars have disagreed.

Some have said: The truth in all such cases is one, and all else is false; however, the one who errs therein is not blameworthy. This is the school of al-Shāfiʿī.

Others have said: Every independent jurist is correct. This is the view of Abū Ḥanīfah, Abū al-Ḥasan al-Ashʿarī, al-Qāḍī Abū Bakr, and most of the theologians (*mutakallimūn*).

Both views have been transmitted from Mālik.

5.4   ON UNCRITICAL ADHERENCE   الباب الرابع: في التقليد

ومعنــاه: قبــول قــول الغير من غيــر دليل، وقد اختلف العلمــاء في جوازه، وفي ذلك تفصيل:

[*Taqlīd* (uncritical adherence):] its meaning is accepting the statement of another without evidence. Scholars have differed regarding its permissibility, and there is detail in that:

أمّا أصول الدين، فمنع أكثر المتكلّمين من التقليد فيها، وأجازه أكثر المحدّثين وغيرهم.

As for the principles of religion, most of the theologians (*mutakallimūn*) prohibited *taqlīd* (uncritical adherence) in them, while most of the ḥadīth scholars (*muḥaddithūn*) and others permitted it.

وأمّــا فــروع الفقه التي علمت من الدين ضــرورةً فلا يجوز التقليد فيها لاشتراك الناس في العلم بها.

As for the branches of jurisprudence that are known from religion by necessity, it is not permissible to practice *taqlīd* in them, due to the commonality of people in knowledge of them.

وأمّا الفروع التي لا تعلم إلّا بالنظر والاســتدلال، فيجوز للعامّيّ الذي لا يعرف طرق الأحكام أن يقلّد عالمًا ويعمل بقوله عند الجمهور.

As for the subsidiary rulings that are not known except through speculative reasoning and inference, it is permissible, according to the majority, for the layperson who does not know the methods of deriving rulings to follow a scholar and act upon his statement.

فروع

الأوّل: يجوز تقليد المذاهب في النوازل والانتقال من مذهب إلى مذهب بثلاثة شروط:

أحدها: أن يعتقد فيمن يقلّده العلم والفضل.

الثاني: لا يتّبع رخص المذاهب.

الثالث: لا يجمـع بين المذاهب علـى وجه يخالف الإجماع، كمَن تزوّج بغير صداق ولا ولي ولا شهود، فإنّ هذه الصورة لم يقل بها أحد.

First Branch: It is permissible to follow the legal schools (*madhāhib*) in novel cases (*nawāzil*) and to move from one school to another under three conditions:

First: That he believes the one he follows to possess knowledge and virtue.

Second: That he does not chase the dispensations of the schools.

Third: That he does not combine between doctrines in a manner that contravenes consensus, such as one who marries without a dower, a guardian, or witnesses – for no one has upheld this configuration.

الثانـي: إذا فعـل المكلّف فعلًا مختلفًا فـي تحريمه غير مقلّد لأحد، فاختلف هل هو آثم بناء على القول بالتحريم، أو غير آثم بناءً على القول بالجواز.

Second Branch: If the legally responsible individual (*mukallaf*) performs an act whose permissibility is disputed, without following any authority, there is disagreement as to whether he is sinful – based on the opinion that it is prohibited – or not sinful – based on the opinion that it is permissible.

الثالـث : يقلّـد غير العلماء فيما يختصّ بهـم مـن المعارف والصنائع، فمِن ذلك تقليد القائف في إلحاق النسـب، وتقليد القاسـم في القسـم، وتقليـد التاجـر في قيـم المتلفات، وتقليد الخارص فيمـا يخرصه، وتقليد الراوي فيما يرويه، وتقليد الجزّار في الذكاة.

Third Branch: He follows non-scholars in that which pertains specifically to them among the sciences and crafts, such as: following the physiognomist (*qāʾif*) in attributing lineage; the divider (*qāsim*) in apportionment; the merchant in valuing damaged goods; the crop estimator (*khāriṣ*) in his estimation; the transmitter (*rāwī*) in what he transmits; and the butcher in ritual slaughter (*dhakāh*).

<table>
<tr><td>5.5</td><td>ON THE FATWĀ AND THE EXAMINATION OF THE ATTRIBUTES OF THE MUFTĪ AND THE MUSTAFTĪ</td><td>الباب الخامس: في الفتوى والنظر في صفة المفتي والمستفتي</td></tr>
</table>

أمّـا المفتي فيجـب أن يجتمع فيه شـروط الاجتهاد علـى القول بوجوب الاجتهـاد. وأمّـا علـى القول بعدم وجوبه فالمفتي ينقـل أقوال إمامه الذي يقلّـد كمالك والشـافعيّ وأبي حنيفة وأحمد بـن حنبل وغيرهم، وهذا هو الشأن في زماننا فيجب أن يحقّق قول إمامه في النازلة التي أفتى بها.

The *muftī* must possess the qualifications of *ijtihād* on the view that *ijtihād* is obligatory. As for the view that it is not obligatory, the *muftī* conveys the opinions of his Imām whom he follows in *taqlīd*, such as Mālik, al-Shāfiʿī, Abū Ḥanīfah, Aḥmad ibn Ḥanbal, and others. This is the prevailing condition in our time, so he must ascertain the opinion of his Imām regarding the specific case in which he issues a *fatwā*.

وأمّا المستفتي فهو العامّيّ الذي لا يعرف طرق الأحكام.

The one seeking a legal opinion (*mustaftī*) is the layperson who does not know the methods of deriving rulings.

وأمّا العالم، فإن كان عالمًا لم يبلغ درجة الاجتهاد جاز له أن يستفتي ويقلّد إمامًا وإن بلغ درجة الاجتهاد، فأكثر أهل السنّة أنّه لا يجوز له التقليد، وأجازه أحمد بن حنبل وإسحاق بن راهويه وسفيان الثوري مطلقًا، وأجازه محمّد بن الحسن أن يقلّد من هو أعلم منه لا من هو مثله.

If the scholar is learned but has not reached the level of *ijtihād*, it is permissible for him to seek a legal opinion and follow an Imām. But if he has reached the level of *ijtihād*, the majority of the Sunnis hold that *taqlīd* is not permissible for him, while Aḥmad ibn Ḥanbal, Isḥāq ibn Rāhwayh, and Sufyān al-Thawrī permitted it unconditionally. Muḥammad ibn al-Ḥasan [al-Shaybānī] permitted him to imitate one who is more learned than himself, but not one who is his equal.

فروع

الفرع الأوّل: لا يجوز للمستفتي أن يستفتي من شاء على الإطلاق، لأنّه ربّما استفتى مَن لا يعرف الفقه، بل يجب أن يتعرّف حال الفقيه في علمه وعدالته ويكفيه في معرفة حاله خبر الواحد.

First Branch: It is not permissible for the *one seeking a fatwā* (*mustaftī*) to ask whomever he wishes without restriction, for he might then ask one who does not know jurisprudence (*fiqh*). Rather, he must ascertain the condition of the jurist in terms of his knowledge and uprightness, and it suffices him in knowing his condition to rely on the report of a single transmitter.

الفرع الثاني: إن وجد المستفتي عالمًا واحدًا قلّده، كان وجد اثنين فأكثر فقيل يقلّد واحد منهم، وقيل يختار أعلمهم وأفضلهم.

Second Branch: If the one seeking a fatwā finds a single scholar, he follows him. If he finds two or more, it is said that he may follow any one of them, and it is also said that he must choose the most learned and virtuous among them.

الفرع الثالث: إن استفتى رجلين فأكثر فاختلفوا في الفتيا، فقيل يأخذ بقــول مَن شـــاء منهــم، وقيل يجتهد فـي أيهم أفضل فيأخــذ بقوله، وقيل يأخذ بالقول الأحوط.

Third Branch: If one consults two or more and they differ in their legal opinion, it is said that he may follow whomever he wishes among them. It is also said that he must exercise judgement as to which of them is superior and follow his opinion. And it is said that he must follow the more precautionary opinion.

5.6 ON THE CONFLICT OF EVIDENCES

الباب السادس: في تعارض الأدلّة

إذا تعارض دليلان فأكثر ففي ذلك ثلاثة طرق:

الأوّل: العمــل بهمــا، وذلك بالجمع بينهما على قدر الإمكان ولو من وجه واحد، وهذا أولى الطرق لأنّه ليس فيه إطراح لأحدهما.

الثانـي: ترجيــح أحدهما علــى الآخر بوجه من وجــوه الترجيح المذكورة بعد.

الثالث: نسخ أحدهما بالآخر وشرط معرفة المتقدّم والمتأخّر منهما.

If two or more proofs conflict, there are three approaches to this:

First: Acting upon both of them, by reconciling them to the extent possible, even if only from one aspect. This is the preferred method, for it does not involve discarding either of them.

Second: Preferentially weighing (*tarjīh*) one of the two over the other by means of one of the aspects of preferential weighing mentioned below.

Third: Abrogating one by means of the other, with the condition of knowing which of the two is antecedent and which is subsequent.

فإن عجـز عـن الجمـع والترجيـح تسـاقط الدليلان ووجـب التوقّف أو تقليـد مجتهد آخر عثر على الترجيح، وقال القاضي أبو بكر بن الطيّب: «يتخيّـر فـي العمل بأيّهما شـاء»، وقال الأبهـريّ: «يتعيّن الحظر»، وقال أبو الفرج: «تتعيّن الإباحة» بناء على أصله أن «الأشياء على الإباحة».

If one is unable to reconcile or preferentially weigh one over the other, the two evidences nullify each other, and suspension of judgement becomes obligatory, or one must follow another independent jurist who has arrived at a preference.

Qāḍī Abū Bakr ibn al-Ṭayyib said: He may choose to act upon whichever of the two he wishes.

Al-Abharī said: Prohibition becomes determinate.

Abū al-Faraj said: Permission becomes determinate – based on his principle that things are originally permitted.

5.7   ON PREFERENTIAL WEIGHING   **الباب السابع: في الترجيح**

اتّفـق جمهـور العلمـاء على القول بالترجيح بين الأدلّة، وأنكره بعض الناس والصحيـح القـول به، وإنّما يتأتّى في المظنونات، وأمّا القطعيّات فلا يتأتّى فيها لتعذّر التفاوت بين القطعيّين، إذ ليس بعض المعلومات أقوى وأغلب من بعض وإن كانت بعضها أجلى وأقرب حصولًا وأشدّ استغناء عن التأمّل.

The majority of scholars agreed on the admissibility of preferential weighing (*tarjīḥ*) between evidences, while some denied it. The correct view is to affirm it.

However, it is only applicable in matters that are presumptive (*ẓanniyyāt*).

It is not applicable to definitives (*qaṭʿiyyāt*) due to the impossibility of disparity between two certainties. For no item of knowledge is stronger or more dominant than another, even if some are clearer, more readily attained, and more independent of reflection.

فإذا تقـرّر هــذا، فلا يخلو أن يكون الدلـيلان المتعارضان قطعيّين، أو
ظنّيّين، أو أحدهما قطعيّ والآخر ظنّيّ:

(١) فإن كانـا قطعيّيـن، كالنصـوص المتواتـرة، فللمجتهـد حالتـان:
الجمع بينهما إن أمكن، والنسخ إن علم التأويل.

(٢) وإن كانـا ظنّيّيـن، كالظواهـر والعمومات ونصـوص أخبار الآحاد
فلها ثلاثة أحوال: الجمع إن أمكن، والنسخ إن علم التاريخ، والترجيح.

(٣) وإن كان أحدهمـا قطعيًّـا والآخـر ظنيًّـا، فإن جهـل التاريخ تعيّن
المعلوم، وإن تأخّر المعلوم نسـخ المظنون، كان تأخّر المظنون لم ينسـخ
المعلوم.

Once this is established, then the two conflicting proofs must be either: both definitive, both presumptive, or one definitive and the other presumptive.

(1) If both are definitive – such as the recurrently mass-transmitted texts – then the independent jurist has two courses: reconciliation between them, if possible; or abrogation, if the chronology[84] is known.

(2) If both are presumptive – such as apparent meanings, generalities, and the explicit texts of solitary reports – then they have three courses: reconciliation, if possible; abrogation, if the chronology is known; and preferential weighing.

(3) If one of the two is definitive and the other presumptive, then: if the chronology is unknown, the definitive is to be adopted; if the definitive is subsequent, it abrogates the presumptive; and if the presumptive is subsequent, it does not abrogate the definitive.

---

84   (Tr:) The Arabic says *interpretation* (*taʾwīl*), which the editor explains as *history* (*tārīkh*) which matches what comes in the next paragraphs.

فروع أربعة

الفـرع الأوّل: إذا تعـارض ظاهـر من الكتاب وظاهر من السـنّة ففي ذلك ثلاثـة أقـوال: قيل يقدّم القرآن، وقيل تقدّم السـنّة لأنّها مفسّـرة للكتاب، وقيل: متوقّف.

First Branch: If the apparent meaning (*ẓāhir*) of the Qurʾān conflicts with the apparent meaning of the Sunnah, there are three opinions on the matter: it is said the Qurʾān is given precedence; it is said the Sunnah is given precedence, for it explains the Book; and it is said one withholds judgement.

الفـرع الثانـي: إذا تعـارض نصّـان، أو ظاهـران وأحدهمـا أقـرب إلى الاحتياط أخذ بالأحوط عند كثير من الفقهاء خلافًا للقاضي أبي بكر.

Second Branch: If two texts, or two apparent meanings, are in conflict, and one of them is closer to precaution, the more precautionary is to be adopted according to many jurists, contrary to the view of Qāḍī Abū Bakr.

الفـرع الثالـث: إذا تعـارض نصّـان، أو ظاهران، وانضـمّ إلى أحدهما قياس يوافقه رجّح على الآخر.

Third Branch: If two texts, or two apparent meanings, are in conflict, and one of them is supported by an analogy that accords with it, it takes precedence over the other.

الفرع الرابع: إذا تعارض الأصل والغالب فاختلف أيّهما يرجّح، وترجيح الغالب أكثر.

Fourth Branch: If the default (*aṣl*) and the prevalent (*ghālib*) are in conflict, there is a difference of opinion as to which takes precedence, though the prevalent is more often given preferential weighing.

5.8 ON THE PREFERENTIAL WEIGHING OF REPORTS

الباب الثامن: في ترجيح الأخبار

وهي إمّا في الإسناد، وإمّا في المتن:

It is either in the chain of transmission (*isnād*), or in the text (*matn*).

فأمّـا الترجيح في الإسـناد فيكون بعشـرين وجهًـا وهي: (١) أن يكون أحدهما يشـهد لهما القرآن أو السـنّة المتواترة أو الإجماع أو دليل العقل للعمل به، (٢) أو يكون في قضيّة مشـهورة والآخر ليس كذلك، (٣) أو يكون رواته أكثر، (٤) أو أحفظ، (٥) أو يكون مسموعًا من النبيّ -صلّى الله عليه وسلّم- والآخر مكتوب عنه،

Preferential weighing in the chain of transmission (*isnād*) occurs in twenty aspects, which are:[85]

1. That one of the two is supported by the Qurʾān, by recurrent mass-transmission from the Sunnah, by consensus, or by a rational proof for acting upon it.
2. That it pertains to a well-known case, while the other does not.
3. That its transmitters are more numerous.
4. That its transmitters are more precise in memory.
5. That it was heard directly from the Prophet (may Allah bless him and grant him peace) while the other was only written from him.

(٦) أو متوقّف على رفعه إليه -صلّى الله عليه وسلّم-، (٧) أو تتوقّف روايتـه علــى إثبات الحكم بـه، (٨) أو يكون راويه صاحب القضيّة، (٩) أو يعضـده إجمـاع أهـل المدينـة على العمـل به، (١٠) أو تكـون روايته أحسن نسقًا،

6. That it depends on being raised to him[86] – may Allah bless him and grant him peace.

---

85   (Tr:) The author lists twenty aspects in continuous prose joined by *aw* ("or"). The segmentation into discrete items is editorial.

86   (Tr:) i.e. a Companion says something that could not be based on his own opinion. See §4.4.3.

7. That its transmission depends on affirming the ruling by it.
8. That its transmitter is the one involved in the case.
9. That it is supported by the consensus of the people of Medina on acting upon it.

(١١) أو يكون سالـمًا من الاضطراب والآخر ليس كذلك، (١٢) أو يكون راويه مـن أكابر الصحابـة، (١٣) أو يكون فقيهًـا، (١٤) أو عالـمًا بالعربيّة، (١٥) أو عرفت عدالته بالاختبار،

10. That its transmission is better in arrangement.
11. That it is free from inconsistency, while the other is not.
12. That its transmitter is among the senior Companions.
13. That its transmitter is a jurist.
14. That its transmitter is knowledgeable in Arabic.
15. That his uprightness is known through testing.

(١٦) أو بتعديـل الجمـع الكثير، (١٧) أو ذكر سـبب عدالته، (١٨) ولـم يختلـط عقلـه في بعض الأوقات، (١٩) أو له اسـم واحد لا يختلط بغيـره، (٢٠) أو يكـون مدنيًّـا أو متأخّـر الإسلام ليعلـم أن مـا رواه غيـر منسوخ.

16. That his uprightness is known through the commendation of a large group.
17. That the reason for his uprightness is mentioned.
18. That his intellect was never impaired at any time.
19. That he has a single name not confused with another.
20. That he is from Medina, or that he was a late convert to Islam, so it is known that what he transmitted is not abrogated.

وأمّا الترجيح في المتن فيكون بخمسة عشر وجهًا وهي: (١-٤) أن يكون نصًّا في المراد، أو سـالـمًا من الاضطراب، أو يكون مسـتقلًّا بنفسه مستغنيًا عن الإضمار أو غير متّفق على تخصيصه، (٥) أو ورد على غير سبب،

Preferential weighing in the text (*matn*) occurs through fifteen aspects, which are:[87]

1–4. That it be explicit in the intended meaning, free from inconsistency, self-sufficient, not requiring ellipsis, or not unanimously agreed upon as restricted in application.

5. That it was revealed without a specific occasion.

(٦) وقضـي بـه على الآخر في موضـع، (٧) أو ورد بعبارات مختلفة لمعنى واحد، (٨) أو يتضمّن نفي النقص عن الصحابة رضي اللَّه عنهم (٩) أو يكون فصيح اللفظ، (١٠) أو لفظه حقيقة،

6. That it was applied as precedent over the other in another context.

7. That it was transmitted in different expressions conveying one meaning.

8. That it entails the negation of deficiency from the Companions – may Allah be pleased with them.

9. That it be eloquent in wording.

10. That its wording be literal.

(١١) أو يـدلّ على المراد من وجهيـن، (١٢) أو تأكّد لفظه بالتكرار (١٣) أو يكون ناقلًا عن حكم العقل، (١٤) أو لم يعمل بعض الصحابة أو السلف على خلافه مع الاطّلاع عليه، (١٥) أو كان ممّا تعمّ به البلوى والآخر ليس كذلك.

11. That it indicates the intended meaning in two ways.

12. That its wording be reinforced by repetition.

13. That it transfers [a matter] from the ruling of the intellect.

14. That none of the Companions or early predecessors acted contrary to it despite being aware of it.

15. That it pertains to a matter of widespread affliction (*ʿumūm balwā*), while the other does not.

---

87   (Tr:) The author lists fifteen aspects in continuous prose joined by *aw* ("or"). The segmentation into discrete items is editorial.

5.9 ON THE PREFERENTIAL WEIGHING OF ANALOGIES	الباب التاسع: في ترجيحات الأقيسة

قـد ذكرنـا في باب القياس أنّ مراتب القياس متفاوتة في القوّة والضعف، وأنّ منه الجليّ والخفيّ، فإذا تعارض قياسان قُدِّم الأقوى على الأضعف، والجلـيّ علـى الخفيّ، والأجلى على ما هـو أقلّ جلاءً منه، ويُقَدَّم قياس العلّة على قياس المناسبة، ويقدّم قياس المناسبة على قياس الشبه.

We have mentioned in the chapter on analogies that the ranks of analogy vary in strength and weakness, and that among them are the manifest and the obscure.[88]

So, when two analogies are in conflict, the stronger is given precedence over the weaker, the manifest over the obscure, and the more manifest over that which is less so.

The analogy of cause (*qiyās ʿillah*) is given precedence over the analogy of suitability (*qiyās munāsabah*), and the analogy of suitability is given precedence over the analogy of resemblance (*qiyās shabah*).

ويترجّح قياس العلّة على قياس العلّة بخمسـة عشـر وجهًا، وهي: (١) النصّ على علّته (٢) أو الاتّفاق على علّته، (٣) أو تكون علّته أقلّ خلافًا، (٤) أو مطّردةً منعكسةً، (٥) أو تشهد لها أصول كثيرة،

The analogy of cause (*qiyās ʿillah*) is given preferential weighing over another analogy of cause in fifteen respects, which are:

1. That its cause is textually explicit.
2. That there is agreement upon its cause.
3. That its cause is less disputed.
4. That it is consistent and reversible.
5. That it is supported by many foundational principles.

---

88   See §4.7.3.

(٦) أو تكون متعدّيةً والأخرى قاصرةً، (٧) أو تعمّ فروعها، (٨) أو هي أعمّ، (٩) أو منتزعة من أصل منصوص عليه، (١٠) أو تكون أقلَّ أوصافًا،

6. That it is transitive, while the other is intransitive.
7. That it encompasses its branches.
8. That it is more general.
9. That it is derived from a textually established source.
10. That it possesses fewer attributes.

(١١) أو تكـون بعـض مقدّماتـه يقينيّـةً، (١٢) أو تكـون علّتـه وصفًا حقيقيًّا، (١٣) أو يكون أحد القياسـين فروعه من أصل جنسه (١٤) أو لا يعـود علـى أصله بالتخصيص، (١٥) أو يكون ثبوت الحكم في أصله أقوى بالإجماع أو بالتواتر والآخر ليس كذلك.

11. That some of its premises are definitive.
12. That its cause is a real attribute.
13. That one of the two analogies has branches stemming from a genus of its base case.
14. That it does not entail specification of its base case.
15. That the establishment of the ruling in its base case is stronger by consensus or by recurrent mass-transmission, while the other is not so.

<table>
<tr><td>5.10</td><td>ON THE CAUSES OF DISAGREEMENT AMONG THE INDEPENDENT JURISTS</td><td>الباب العاشر: في أسباب الخلاف بين المجتهدين</td></tr>
</table>

وهي ستّة عشر بالاستقراء، على أنّ هذا الباب انفردنا بذكره لعظم فائدته، ولم يذكره أهل الأصول في كتبهم.

They are sixteen by induction, given that we have singled out this chapter for mention due to its great benefit, while the scholars of legal theory (*uṣūl*) did not mention it in their books.

السـبب الأوّل: تعـارض الأدلّـة. وهــو أغلب أسـباب الـخلاف، وقد تكلّمنا عليه في بابه.

First Reason: The conflict of evidences is the predominant cause of disagreement, and we have discussed it in its proper section.[89]

السبب الثانـي: الجهـل بالدليـل. وأكثر ما يجـيء في الأخبـار لأنّ بعـض المجتهدين يبلغه الحديـث فيقضي به، وبعضهم لا يبلغه فيقضي بخلافه، فينبغي للمجتهد أن يكثر من حفظ الحديث وروايته لتكون أقواله علـى مقتضى الأحاديث النبويّة، ولذلك كثرت مخالفة أبي حنيفة رحمه اللَّه للحديـث لقلّة روايته له فرجع إلى القياس، بخلاف أحمد بن حنبل فإنّه كان متّسـع الروايـة للحديث فاعتمد عليه وتـرك القياس، وأمّا مالك والشـافعيّ فإنّهما أخذا بالطرفين، وقد قال الشـافعيّ: «إذا صحّ الحديث فهو مذهبي».

Second Reason: Ignorance of the proof.

This occurs most frequently in the transmitted reports, because some independent jurists receive a ḥadīth and issue judgement accordingly, while others do not receive it and issue judgement contrary to it. Therefore, it is incumbent upon the independent jurist to increase in memorisation and transmission of ḥadīth, so that his statements conform to the purport of the Prophetic reports.

For this reason, Abū Ḥanīfah – may Allah have mercy on him – frequently opposed ḥadīth due to his limited transmission thereof,[90] and thus resorted to analogy. In contrast, Aḥmad ibn Ḥanbal had a wide transmission of ḥadīth, so he relied upon it and abandoned analogy.

---

89   See §5.10.

90   (Tr:) It is not so much that his transmission was limited, but that he had reason to question the reliability of so many.

Mālik and al-Shāfiʿī adopted both approaches. Al-Shāfiʿī said: "If the ḥadīth is authentic, then it is my school."[91]

السبب الثالث: الاختلاف في صحّة نقل الحديث بعد بلوغه إلى كلّ مجتهد، إلّا أنّ مِنهم مَن صحّ عنده فعمل بمقتضاه، ومِنهم من لم يصحّ عنده إمّا لقدح في سنده، أو لتشديده في شروط الصحّة، كثيرًا ما يجري ذلك لمالك رحمه اللّه فإنّه مِن أشدّ أهل العلم تحفّظًا في نقل الحديث.

Third Reason: The disagreement concerning the reliability of the transmission of ḥadīth after it reached each independent jurist, [where] some among them deemed it sound and acted accordingly, while others did not deem it sound – either due to a flaw in its chain of transmission, or due to their stringency in the conditions of soundness.

This frequently occurred with Mālik – may Allah have mercy on him – for he was among the most scrupulous of the scholars in transmitting ḥadīth.

السبب الرابع: الاختلاف في نوع الدليل هل يحتجّ به أم لا؟ فهذا السبب أوجب كثيرًا من الخلاف، وذلك كعمل أهل المدينة وهو حجّة عند مالك فعمل بمقتضاه، وليس حجّة عند غيره فلم يعملوا به، كالقياس وهو حجّة عند الجمهور فعملوا به. وليس حجّةً عند الظاهريّة فلم يعملوا به.

وقد استوفينا الكلام على ذلك كلّه في فنّ الأدلّة.

Fourth Reason: The disagreement concerning the type of proof – whether it is adduced as probative (*yuḥtajj bihi*) or not. This cause has led to much disagreement.

---

91   (Tr:) He said this about specific issues; it is not a general rule that allows one to pick whatever *ṣaḥīḥ* hadith they want simply because it is *ṣaḥīḥ*. Imām al-Subkī has a book dedicated to clarifying this issue. While Ibn Juzay may be excused from being aware of it, the same cannot be said of contemporaries who apply Imām al-Shāfiʿī's statement to everything.

For example, the practice of the people of Medina (*'amal ahl al-Madīnah*) is considered authoritative by Mālik, so he acted in accordance with it. It is not considered authoritative by others, so they did not act upon it. Likewise, analogy is authoritative according to the majority, so they acted upon it. It is not authoritative according to the Ẓāhiriyyah, so they did not act upon it.

We have fully addressed all of that in the discipline of evidences.[92]

السبب الخامس: الاختلاف في قاعدة من الأصول ينبني عليها الاختلاف في الفروع كحمل المطلق على المقيَّد وشبه ذلك.

Fifth Reason: The divergence concerning a foundational principle upon which disagreement in subsidiary matters is based, such as construing the absolute in light of the qualified and the like.

السبب السادس: الاختلاف في القراءات في القرآن، فيأخذ مجتهد بقراءة، ويأخذ غيره بأخرى، كقوله تعالى: ﴿وَامْسَحُوا بِرُؤُوسِكُمْ وَأَرْجُلَكُمْ﴾ [المائدة ٦] قرئ بالنصب فاقتضى غسل الرِّجْلَيْنِ لعطفه على الأيدي، وقرئ بالخفض فاقتضى مسحهما لعطفه على الرؤوس إلّا أن يتأوَّل على غير ذلك.

Sixth Reason: The divergence in Qurʾānic readings: One independent jurist adopts one reading, while another adopts a different one.

For example, His saying, exalted is He: "And wipe your heads and your feet."[93] It is recited in the accusative, which entails washing the feet due to its being conjoined to the hands; and it is recited in the genitive, which entails wiping them due to its being conjoined to the heads – unless it be interpreted otherwise.

---

92   See §4.1.

93   Qurʾān, 5:6.

السبب السابع: في اختلاف الرواية في ألفاظ الحديث، كقوله -صلّى اللَّـه عليـه وسـلّم-: «ذَكَاةُ الْجَنِينِ ذَكَاةُ أُمِّهِ» روي بالرفع فأخذ به مالك والشافعيّ، وبالنصب فأخذ به أبو حنيفة.

Seventh Reason: The variation in the wording of the ḥadīth transmission.

Such as his saying (may Allah bless him and grant him peace) "The slaughtering of the foetus is the slaughtering of its mother."[94] It was transmitted in the nominative, and Mālik and al-Shāfiʿī acted upon it; and in the accusative, and Abū Ḥanīfah acted upon it.

السـبب الثامـن: اخـتلاف وجه الإعراب مع اتّفاق القـراء في الرواية، مثل قوله عليه السلام: «أكْلُ كُلِّ ذِي نَابٍ مِنَ السِّبَاعِ حَرَامٌ»، فبعضهم جعـل الأكل مصـدرًا مضافًـا إلى المفعول، فحرم أكل السباع، وبعضهم جعلـه مضافًـا إلـى الفاعل بعد قوله تعالى: ﴿وَمَا أَكَلَ السَّبُعُ﴾ [المائدة ٣] فأجاز أكل السباع.

Eighth Reason: The disagreement concerning the aspect of grammatical parsing despite agreement of the reciters in transmission.

---

94   From Jābir: al-Dārimī, 1979; Abū Dāwūd, 2828; al-Baghawī,_ al-Jaʿdiyyāt_, 2653; al-Ḥākim, 7109 – he said: ṣaḥīḥ on the condition of Muslim; al-Bayhaqī, 19272.

From Abū Ayyūb: al-Ṭabarānī, 4010 – al-Haythamī said: in it is Muḥammad ibn Abī Laylā, who has poor memory but is trustworthy; al-Ḥākim, 7112.

From Abū Saʿīd: Aḥmad, 11361; Abū Dāwūd, 2827; al-Tirmidhī, 1476 – he said: ḥasan ṣaḥīḥ; Ibn Mājah, 3199; Abū Yaʿlā, 1206; Ibn al-Jārūd, 900; Ibn Ḥibbān, 5889; al-Dāraquṭnī; al-Ḥākim, 7112; al-Bayhaqī, 19276.

From Abū Umāmah and Abū al-Dardāʾ: al-Ṭabarānī, 7498 – al-Haythamī said: in it is Bishr ibn ʿUmārah, who has been deemed trustworthy though there is weakness in him.

From Abū Hurayrah: al-Ḥākim, 7110; al-Dāraquṭnī.

From Kaʿb ibn Mālik: al-Ṭabarānī, *al-Kabīr*, 157; al-Ṭabarānī, *al-Awsaṭ*, 3711 – al-Haythamī said: in it is Ismāʿīl ibn Muslim, who is weak.

Such as his saying (may Allah bless him and grant him peace) "The eating of every beast possessing fangs is forbidden."[95] Some considered "eating" (*akl*) a verbal noun annexed to the object, thus prohibiting the eating of predatory beasts. Others considered it annexed to the subject, in view of His saying, exalted is He: "And what the beast has eaten,"[96] thereby permitting the eating of predatory beasts.

السبب التاسع: كون اللفظ مشتركًا بين معنيين، فأخذ بعض المحدثين بمعنى، وغيره بمعنى، كقوله تعالى: ﴿ثَلَاثَةَ قُرُوءٍ﴾ [البقرة ٢٢٨] فحملها مالك والشافعيّ على الإطهار وأبو حنيفة على الحيض لاشتراك اللفظ بين المعنيين.

Ninth Reason: The disagreement due to a word being equivocal between two meanings: Some scholars of ḥadīth took it in one sense, and others in another.

Such as His saying, exalted is He: "Three *qurū*."[97] Mālik and al-Shāfiʿī construed it as purification (*ṭuhr*), while Abū Ḥanīfah construed it as menstruation (*ḥayḍ*), due to the word being equivocal between the two meanings.

السبب العاشر: الاختلاف في حمل اللفظ على العموم أو الخصوص مثل قوله تعالى: ﴿وَأَنْ تَجْمَعُوا بَيْنَ الْأُخْتَيْنِ﴾ [النساء ٢٣] يحمل على الزوجات والمملوكات أو على الزوجات خاصّة.

Tenth Reason: The disagreement concerning whether a term is to be construed as general or particular.

Such as His saying, exalted is He: "And that you combine between two sisters."[98] It may be construed to include wives and bondwomen, or to wives alone.

---

95 From Abū Hurayrah: al-Shāfiʿī; Mālik, 1060; Ibn Mājah, 3233; Abū ʿAwānah, 7602; Ibn Ḥibbān, 5278; al-Bayhaqī, 19139; al-Daylamī, 1699.

96 Qurʾān, 5:3.

97 Qurʾān, 2:228.

98 Qurʾān, 4:23.

السبب الحادي عشــر: الاختلاف في حمل اللفظ على الحقيقة أو
على المجاز.

Eleventh Reason: The disagreement concerning whether a term
is to be construed according to the literal or to the figurative.

السبب الثاني عشــر: الاختلاف هل في الكلام مضمر أم لا. كقوله
تعالى: ﴿فَمَنْ كَانَ مِنْكُمْ مَرِيضًا أَوْ عَلَى سَفَرٍ فَعِدَّةٌ مِنْ أَيَّامٍ أُخَرَ﴾ [البقرة
١٨٤] فعله الجمهور على إضمار «فأفطر» خلافًا للظاهريّة.

Twelfth Reason: The disagreement concerning whether there is
an ellipsis in the wording or not

Such as His saying, exalted is He: "So whoever among you is ill or
on a journey, then a number of other days."[99] The majority construed
it with the ellipsis "then he broke the fast," contrary to the Ẓāhiriyyah.

السبب الثالـث عشــر: الاختلاف هـل الحكم منسـوخ أم لا؟ وهذا
أوجب كثيرًا من الخلاف.

Thirteenth Reason: The disagreement concerning whether a ruling
is abrogated or not. This has led to much disagreement.

السبب الرابع عشر: الاختلاف في حمل الأمر على الوجوب أو على
الندب، وهذا أيضًا أوجب كثيرًا من الخلاف.

Fourteenth Reason: The disagreement concerning whether a
command is to be construed as obligation or recommendation. This
too has led to much disagreement.

السبب الخامس عشــر: الاختلاف في حمل النهي على التحريم أو
على الكراهة.

---

99   Qurʾān, 2:184.

Fifteenth Reason: The disagreement concerning whether a prohibition is to be construed as prohibition or reprehensibility.

السبب السادس عشر: الاختلاف في فعل النبيّ -صلّى الله عليه وسلّم- هل يحمل على الوجوب أو على الندب أو الإباحة.

Sixteenth Reason: The disagreement concerning the action of the Prophet (may Allah bless him and grant him peace) whether it is to be construed as obligation, recommendation, or permissibility.

[CLOSING]

كملت المقدّمة المباركة بحمد اللَّه وحسن عونه، وصلّى اللَّه على سيّدنا
ومولانا محمّد وآله وصحبه وسلّم، والحمد للَّه ربّ العالمين

Thus is completed the blessed introduction by the praise of Allah and His good aid. May Allah send blessings upon our master and our patron Muḥammad, and upon his family and his companions, and grant them peace. And praise be to Allah, Lord of the worlds. ۞

BIOGRAPHICAL NOTES

[التراجم]

Basic information about scholars mentioned in this book is provided below to facilitate locating them in more comprehensive biographical works. Entries are in alphabetical order, ignoring the initial "al-" and diacritics. Each begins with the person's name and lineage, usually followed by their Hijri dates of birth and death (in parentheses, if known), and then brief biographical information. Titles and nicknames will come first in cases where an individual is best known through them. Cross references are also given (separated by an equals sign). Most honourifics have been omitted for the sake of brevity; readers are encouraged to add them as they read.

al-Abharī Muḥammad ibn ʿAbd Allāh ibn Muḥammad ibn Ṣāliḥ Abū Bakr al-Tamīmī (289–375 AH/902–986 CE). The leading Mālikī scholar of Iraq. He was born in Abhar and settled in Baghdad. He declined the judgeship when it was offered to him. He authored works in defence of the Mālikī school and in refutation of its opponents, including *al-Radd ʿalā al-Muzanī*. Among his other works are *Kitāb al-Uṣūl, Ijmāʿ* Ahl al-Madīnah, *and* Faḍl al-Madīnah ʿalā Makkah*.

Abū al-Faraj al-Mālikī ʿUmar ibn Muḥammad (d. 331 AH/943 CE). A jurist and legal theorist of the Mālikī school. His works include *al-Ḥāwī fī al-Fiqh* and *al-Lumaʿ* fī Uṣūl al-Fiqh*.

Abū Ḥanīfah al-Nuʿmān ibn Thābit ibn Zūwṭa al-Taymī al-Kūfī (80–150 AH/699–767 CE). The great legist and founder of the school bearing his name. He was known for his noble character, sound intellect, and beautiful appearance. Imām al-Shāfiʿī praised him saying: "All scholars depend on Abū Ḥanīfa in *fiqh*."

Abū Ḥāmid al-Ghazālī Muḥammad ibn Muḥammad ibn Muḥammad al-Ṭūsī al-Shāfiʿī, Ḥujjat al-Islām (450–505 AH/1058–1111 CE). One of the foremost authorities in jurisprudence, legal theory, mysticism, and *kalām* in Islam. A prominent student of Imām al-Ḥaramayn, he taught at the Niẓāmiyyah in Baghdad before leaving to pursue asceticism and travel, later returning to Ṭūs to focus on writing and worship. His works include *Iḥyāʾ* ʿUlūm al-Dīn, al-Mustaṣfā, Tahāfut al-Falāsifah, *and* al-Munqidh min al-Ḍalāl*.

Abū al-Ḥasan al-AshʿarīʿAlī ibn Ismāʿīl ibn Isḥāq (260–324 AH/874–936 CE). Founder of the Ashʿarī school of theology. Born in Basra, he initially followed the Muʿtazilī school under his teacher Abū ʿAlī al-Jubbāʾī before publicly renouncing it and dedicating himself to refuting their doctrines. His works are said to number fifty-five, including *Maqālāt al-Islāmiyyīn, al-Ibānah ʿan Uṣūl al-Diyānah, al-Lumaʿ*, and *Istīḥsān al-Khawḍ fī al-Kalām*. He died in Baghdad.

Abū al-Maʿālī al-JuwaynīʿAbd al-Malik ibnʿAbd Allāh ibn Yūsuf, Imām al-Ḥaramayn (419–478 AH/1028–1085 CE). The most knowledge-able of all late scholars of the Shāfiʿī school. Born in Juwayn near Naysābūr, he travelled to Baghdad and the Ḥijāz before returning to Naysābūr, where Niẓām al-Mulk established the Niẓāmiyyah school under his leadership. He became a central figure in consolidating Ashʿarī theology. His principal works include *al-Irshād, al-Shāmil, al-Burhān, Ghiyāth al-Umam*, and *Nihāyat al-Maṭlab*.

Abū al-Walīd al-Bājī Sulaymān ibn Khalaf ibn Saʿd al-Tujībī al-Qurṭubī (403–474 AH/1012–1081 CE). A major Mālikī jurist and *ḥadīth* schol-ar of al-Andalus. Born in Beja, he travelled to the Ḥijāz, Baghdad, Mosul, Damascus, and Aleppo over thirteen years in pursuit of knowledge, and excelled in *ḥadīth, fiqh, uṣūl*, and dialectics. He held judgeships in various parts of al-Andalus. His most famous work is *al-Muntaqā*, a commentary on Mālik's *al-Muwaṭṭaʾ*. Other works include *al-Taʿdīl wa-l-Tajrīḥ li-man rawā ʿanhu al-Bukhārī fī al-Ṣaḥīḥ* and *Iḥkām al-Fuṣūl fī Aḥkām al-Uṣūl*. He died in Almería.

Abū Yūsuf Yaʿqūb ibn Ibrāhīm ibn Ḥabīb (113–182 AH/731–798 CE). A legist and *ḥadīth* master. He studied under Imām Abū Ḥanīfah and was the first to spread his school and the first to record *fiqh*. He was appointed judge during the caliphates of al-Mahdī, al-Hādī, and al-Rashīd.

Aḥmad ibn Ḥanbal AbūʿAbd Allāh al-Shaybānī (164–241 AH/780–855 CE). The founder of the Ḥanbalī school and one of the greatest *imāms* of *ḥadīth*. He is renowned for his steadfastness during the trial (*miḥnah*) and for his adherence to the *Sunnah*. Al-Shāfiʿī said: "I left Baghdad without leaving behind anyone more knowledgeable, more scrupulous, or more pious than Aḥmad ibn Ḥanbal."

al-ʿAnbarī Ubayd Allāh ibn al-Ḥasan ibn al-Ḥusayn al-Tamīmī (105–168 AH/723–785 CE). A jurist and *ḥadīth* scholar of Basra. Ibn Ḥibbān described him as among its leading figures in jurisprudence and knowledge. He served as judge of Basra from 157 AH until his dismissal in 166 AH, the year of his death.

al-Bāqillānī Abū Bakr Muḥammad ibn al-Ṭayyib ibn Muḥammad ibn Jaʿfar (338–403 AH/950–1013 CE). A prominent judge and leading figure in the Ashʿarī school. Born in Basra and died in Baghdad. His notable works include *al-Inṣāf*, *al-Tamhīd*, *al-Hidāyah*, and *Iʿjāz al-Qurʾān*.

al-Daqqāq Abū ʿAlī al-Ḥasan ibn ʿAlī al-Naysābūrī al-Shāfiʿī (d. 405 AH/1015 CE). A leading Sufi master and Shāfiʿī jurist of Naysābūr. He studied *fiqh* under al-Qaffāl and al-Ḥuṣrī, excelled in *uṣūl* and Arabic, then turned to *taṣawwuf* under al-Naṣrābādhī. Al-Qushayrī, author of the famous *Risālah*, was his student and son-in-law.

Dāwūd al-Ẓāhirī Dāwūd ibn ʿAlī ibn Khalaf Abū Sulaymān (201–270 AH/816–884 CE). A *mujtahid imām* and founder of the Ẓāhirī school of jurisprudence. He adhered to the literal meaning of the Qurʾān and *Sunnah*, and avoided interpretation and analogical reasoning.

Fakhr al-Dīn al-Rāzī Muḥammad ibn ʿUmar ibn al-Ḥasan al-Taymī al-Bakrī (544–606 AH/1150–1210 CE). Renowned for his encyclopaedic intellect and disputative prowess, he authored numerous influential works in rational theology, including *Maḥṣūl Afkār al-Mutaqaddimīn wa-l-Mutaʾakhkhirīn*, *Maʿālim Uṣūl al-Dīn*, and *al-Mabāḥith al-Mashriqiyyah*. **Note:** Also known as Fakhr al-Dīn ibn al-Khaṭīb (his father was known as Khaṭīb al-Rayy).

Ibn Ḥazm ʿAlī ibn Aḥmad ibn Saʿīd al-Ẓāhirī Abū Muḥammad (384–456 AH/994–1064 CE). The foremost scholar of al-Andalus in his age and one of the leading *imāms* of Islam. He and his father before him held the vizierate, but he turned to scholarship and became a *ḥāfiẓ* and jurist who derived rulings directly from the Qurʾān and *Sunnah* according to the Ẓāhirī school. His son reported that approximately four hundred volumes in his father's handwriting were collected from his works, comprising some eighty thousand leaves. His major works include *al-Muḥallā*, *al-Fiṣal fī al-Milal* *wa-l-Ahwāʾ** wa-l-Niḥal, al-Iḥkām li-Uṣūl al-Aḥkām, *and* Jamharat Ansāb al-ʿArab*. He was expelled from his homeland due to opposition from the jurists of his time, and died in exile at his estate in the countryside of Labla.

Isḥāq ibn Rāhwayh Isḥāq ibn Ibrāhīm ibn Makhlad al-Ḥanẓalī al-Marwazī Abū Yaʿqūb (161–238 AH/778–853 CE). A major *ḥadīth* master and jurist. Aḥmad ibn Ḥanbal said: "I know of no one in Iraq who is his equal." Abū Zurʿah said: "No one with a stronger memory has been seen." He is reported to have memorised seventy thousand *ḥadīths* and to have dictated his *tafsīr* entirely from memory. He met al-Shāfiʿī and debated with him in Mecca, after which he became one of his companions. He died in Naysābūr.

al-Jāḥiẓ Abū ʿUthmān ʿAmr ibn Baḥr ibn Maḥbūb al-Kinānī (163–255 AH/780–869 CE). Leader of the al-Jāḥiẓiyyah branch of the Muʿtazilah. He authored numerous works, including *al-Ḥayawān*, *al-Bayān wa-l-Tabyīn*, and *Akhlāq al-Mulūk*.

Muḥammad ibn al-Ḥasan al-Shaybānī ibn Firqad Abū ʿAbd Allāh (131–189 AH/749–805 CE). An *imām* who studied under Abū Ḥanīfah and then under Abū Yūsuf. His books include *al-Jāmiʿ** al-Kabīr* and *al-Jāmiʿ** al-Ṣaghīr*.

Muways ibn ʿImrān Abū ʿImrān. A Muʿtazilī theologian of the seventh *ṭabaqah*. He was widely learned in *kalām* and jurisprudence, and held the view of *irjāʾ*. Al-Jāḥiẓ mentioned him in *Uṣūl al-Futyā* and related a number of his opinions. Among his views was that it is permissible for Allah to delegate legal rulings to the Prophet (may Allah bless him and give him peace) and the scholars of his community, if He knows they will be correct.

al-Qarāfī Abū al-ʿAbbās Shihāb al-Dīn Aḥmad ibn Idrīs (626–684 AH/1228–1285 CE). A distinguished Mālikī jurist, Ashʿarī theologian, and expert in legal theory, based in Cairo. His works include *Anwār al-Burūq fī Anwāʾ** al-Furūq, al-Dhakhīrah, al-Yawāqīt fī Aḥkām al-Mawāqīt, *and* Nafāʾis al-Uṣūl fī Sharḥ al-Maḥṣūl*.

Sufyān al-Thawrī Sufyān ibn Saʿīd ibn Masrūq Abū ʿAbd Allāh (97–161 AH/716–778 CE). The premier master of *ḥadīth*, jurisprudence, and piety for his time. He is, with Abū Ḥanīfah, the chief representative of the School of Kūfa. Aḥmad called him the *imām* par excellence, and Ibn al-Mubārak said: "I learned from eleven hundred *shaykhs*, but none better than Sufyān."

INDEX

[فهرس المصطلحات والأعلام]

This index covers both technical terms and proper names, interfiled in a single alphabetical sequence. Terms are followed by their Arabic transliterations in italics. Names are entered without transliterations.

Section references follow the numbering system described in the Translator's Preface, in which each art (*fann*) corresponds to a chapter, each *bāb* to a section, and each *faṣl* to a subsection. **Bold** section numbers indicate where a term is formally defined. Transliteration follows the conventions used throughout the translation; the definite article *al-* is ignored for the purposes of alphabetical ordering, as is the letter *ʿayn*.

analogy by suitability *(qiyās munā-sabah)* – §4.7.3, 4.10, 5.9

analogy of resemblance *(qiyās shabah)* – §4.7.3, 5.9

al-ʿAnbarī – §5.3

apodosis *(ijzāʾ al-sharṭ)* – §1.10

apparent *(ẓāhir)* – §2.6.1, 4.3, 4.4.3

assent *(taṣdīq)* – §1.1, 4.4

auditory proof *(samʿī)* – §1.3

B

badness *(qabīḥ)* – §3.6

al-Bāqillānī [al-Qāḍī Abū Bakr] – §2.3.3, 2.4.2, 2.9.2, 5.3, 5.6

blocking the means *(sadd al-dharāʾiʿ)* – §4.1, 4.10

bounded particular *(juzʾiyyah maḥṣūrah)* – §1.10

bounded universal *(kulliyyah maḥṣūrah)* – §1.10

C

cause *(sabab)* – §2.2.2, 3.7

cause *(ʿillah)* – §1.10, 4.7.3, 4.7.4, 5.9

circularity *(dawr)* – §1.1, 1.2

clarified *(mubayyan)* – §2.6.1

classification of the operative cause *(taqsīm al-manāṭ)* – §4.7.3

communal prescription *(farḍ kifāyah)* – §3.3

conception *(taṣawwur)* – §1.1, 1.6

conclusion *(natījah)* – §1.8, 1.10

concomitance *(talāzum)* – §4.8

concomitant antecedent *(malzūm)* – §1.10, **4.8**

concomitant consequent *(lāzim)* – §1.2, 1.5, 1.10, **4.8**

concordant inferred meaning *(mafhūm al-muwāfaqah)* – §2.7

condition *(sharṭ)* – §2.3.2, 2.3.3, 2.5.1, 2.10, 3.4, **3.7**

conditional conjoining *(sharṭī muttaṣil)* – §1.10

conditional disjoining *(sharṭī munfaṣil)* – §1.10

consensus *(ijmāʿ)* – §1.3, 2.3.2, 4.1, 4.5.2, 4.6, 4.6.1, 4.6.2, 4.7, 4.7.4, 5.2, 5.3, 5.8

consequent *(tālī)* – §1.10

construal *(ḥaml)* – §2, **2.1**, 2.5.2, 2.9.1, 4.7.1

contradictories *(naqīḍān)* – §1.7

contradictory propositions *(qaḍiyyatān mutanāqiḍatān)* – §1.10

contraries *(ḍiddān)* – §1.7, 2.9.2

contrary sense *(mafhūm al-mukhālafah)* – §2.7

convention *(waḍʿ)* – §2, **2.1**

convention *(ʿurf)* – §2.2.1, 2.3.2, 2.8.1, 4.10, 5.8

corruption *(fasād)* – §2.9.2, **3.5**

custom *(ʿādah)* – §2.3.2, 4.3, **4.10**

customs *(ʿawāʾid)* – §4.1, **4.10**

D

Al-Daqqāq – §2.7.

Dāwūd al-Ẓāhirī – §4.6.1

decreed *(maḥtum)* – §3.3

deficiency of the cause *(quṣūr al-ʿillah)* – §4.7.4

definite *(maʿrifah)* – §1.6

delusion *(wahm)* – §1.1

delusives *(wahmiyyāt)* – §1.3

demonstration *(burhān)* – §1.8, 1.9

derivation of the operative cause *(takhrīj al-manāṭ)* – §4.7.3

descriptive definition *(rasm)* – §1.2

dialectical reasoning *(jadal)* – §1.9

differents *(khilāfān)* – §1.7

discretionary obligation *(wājib mukhayyar)* – §3.3

disobedience *(maʿṣiyah)* – §3.3

disparate *(mutabāyin)* – §1.4, 1.7

dispensation *(rukhṣah)* – §3.5

distinction *(farq)* – §4.7.4

doubt *(shakk)* – §1.1

due *(mustaḥaqq)* – §2.10, 3.3

E

elimination and division *(sabr wa-taqsīm)* – §1.10, 4.8

elliptical implication of the discourse *(laḥn al-khiṭāb)* – §2.7

ends *(maqāṣid)* – §3.9

equivocal *(mushtarak)* – §1.4, 2.8.1

evil deed *(sayyiʾah)* – §3.3

exception *(istithnāʾ)* – §2.3.2, 2.3.3, 2.4.1, 2.4.2

expanded obligation *(muwassaʿ)* – §3.3

explicit text *(naṣṣ)* – §2.6.1, 4.1, 4.3, 4.4.3, 4.7, 4.7.2, 4.7.4, 5.9

F

Fakhr al-Dīn [al-Rāzī; Ibn al-Khaṭīb] – §1.5, 2.8.1, 2.8.2, 2.9.2, 3.4, 4.4.1

figurative *(majāz)* – §2.1, 2.2.1, 2.2.2, 2.8.1, 2.8.2

forbidden *(mamnūʿ)* – §3.3

G

general *(ʿāmm)* – §2.3.1

generality *(ʿumūm)* – §2.3, 2.3.1–2.3.3, 2.8.1

goodness *(ḥasan)* – §3.6

gradational *(mushakkik)* – §1.4

H

Ḥanafīs – §3.3, 4.7.3, 4.7.4, 4.9

I

Ibn ʿAbbās – §2.4.2

Ibn Ḥazm – §4.4.1

Ibn Juzayy – §0

Ibrāhīm al-Khalīl – §4.3

ignorance *(jahl)* – §1.1, 5.10

imitator *(muqallid)* – §0.1, 4.6.1

immediate *(ḍarūrī)* – §1.3, 5.3

impediment *(māniʿ)* – §3.7

import of the discourse *(faḥwā al-khiṭāb)* – §2.7

Muways ibn ʿImrān – §4.10

O

obligation *(ʿazīmah)* – §3.5

obligatory *(wājib)* – §2.9.1, **3.1**, 3.3, 3.5, 3.9, 5.1

one seeking a fatwā *(mustaftī)* – §5.5

one upon whom the judgement is made *(maḥkūm ʿalayh)* – §1.10

P

part *(juzʾ)* – §1.5, **1.6**, 2.2.2

particular *(juzʾī)* – §1.6

particularity *(juzʾiyyah)* – §1.6

pattern of opposition *(namṭ al-taʿānud)* – §1.10

performance *(adāʾ)* – §3.5

permissible *(mubāḥ)* – §2.9.1, **3.1**, 3.3, 4.4.2, 5.6

personal *(shakhṣiyyah)* – §1.10

poetry *(shiʿr)* – §1.9

consensus of the four caliphs *(ijmāʿ al-khulafāʾ al-arbaʿah)* – §4.1, 4.6.2

consensus of the people of Kūfah *(ijmāʿ ahl al-Kūfah)* – §4.1, 4.6.2

consensus of the people of Medina *(ijmāʿ ahl al-Madīnah)* – §4.1, 4.6.2, 5.8

consensus of the Prophet's family *(ijmāʿ al-ʿitrah)* – §4.6.2

consensus of the ten Companions *(ijmāʿ al-ʿasharah min al-ṣaḥābah)* – §4.1

practice of the people of Medina *(ʿamal ahl al-Madīnah)* – §4.1, 5.10

predicate *(khabar)* – §1.10, 2.9.1

predicate *(maḥmūl)* – §1.10

predicative *(ḥamlī)* – §1.10

preference for the lighter option *(al-akhaf bi-l-akhaf)* – §4.1, **4.9**

premise *(muqaddamah)* – §1.8–**1.10**

prescribed *(farḍ)* – §3.3

presumption *(ẓann)* – §0.1, **1.1**, 1.3, 1.8, 1.9, 2.4.1, 4.4.1, 4.4.2, 5.7, 5.10

presumption of continuity *(istiṣḥāb)* – §4.1, **4.9**

presumptive non-liability *(barāʾah aṣliyyah)* – §4.1, **4.9**

primary convention *(waḍʿ awwalī)* – §**2.1**

prohibited *(ḥarām)* – §2.9.2, **3.1**, **3.3**, 3.5, 3.9

proof *(dalīl)* – §0.1, 0.2, 1.3, 2.3.3, 3.3, 4, 4.1, 4.6.1, 4.6.2, 4.7.2, 4.8, 4.9, 5.4, 5.6–5.8, 5.10

proof of the cause *(burhān al-ʿillah)* – §1.10

proposition *(qaḍiyyah)* – §1.10

proscribed *(maḥẓūr)* – §2.9.1, 5.6

public interest *(maṣlaḥah)* – §4.1, 4.7.3, **4.10**

DETAILED TABLE OF CONTENTS

المُحْتَوَيَاتُ المفصلة

Also from Islamosaic

Ark of Salvation

Connecting to the Quran

Etiquette with the Quran

Infamies of the Soul

Hadith Nomenclature Primers

Hanbali Acts of Worship

Ibn Juzay's Sufic Exegesis

Sharḥ Al-Waraqāt

Shaykh al-Sulamī's Waṣiyyah

The Accessible Conspectus

The Correct Approach to 'Unpacking The Select Creed'

The Encompassing Epistle

The Evident Memorandum

The Ladder to Success in Truly Loving Allah Paperback

The Ultimate Conspectus